Mercier Press

PO Box 5 5 French Church Street Cork

16 Hume Street Dublin 2

Trade enquiries to CMD Distribution

55A Spruce Avenue Stillorgan Industrial Park

Blackrock County Dublin

First published 1996

©Kevin Rafter 1996

A CIP record for this book is available from the British Library.

ISBN 1 85635 141 6

10 9 8 7 6 5 4 3 2 1

Cover photos courtesy of RTE

Cover design by Bluett

Typeset by Richard Parfrey

Printed in Ireland by ColourBooks Baldoyle Dublin 13

CONTENTS

ACKNOWLEDGEMENTS

Many people deserve acknowledgement for helping in the publication of this book. I would like to thank the staff of the National Library, RTÉ Library and the library of Trinity College Dublin. Fianna Fáil Headquarters were of assistance in providing access to that party's historical archives. Many of those who were closely associated with Clann na Poblachta are now deceased. However, a valuable record of the party's achievements remains in party documents and in contemporary reports in the national and local newspapers. A number of RTÉ documentaries provide a vital historical record of the careers of people like Noël Browne, Seán MacBride and indeed of the development of Clann itself. I am grateful to Dr Browne for his time and recollections. Other former members to whom I spoke, including George Lawlor, also provided information and stories.

My thanks also go to friends and family who were supportive while the book was being written. The staff at Marino/Mercier deserve special mention for their time and enthusiasm. Finally, special thanks to my wife, Oorla, to whom this book is dedicated.

INTRODUCTION

It is never easy to establish a new political party. Since 1921 few of those who have attempted to do so have succeeded in the long term. Whatever happened to parties such as Clann Éireann, Irish Workers' League, National League, Córas na Poblachta, Aontacht Éireann, Ailtirí na hAiseirghe or the National Progressive Democratic Party?

Indeed, over the past seventy-five years the Irish political system as represented by its main parties has remained largely unchanged. However, there has been the beginning of a transformation in recent years. Since 1987 most political parties in Dáil Éireann have played some role in government. Minority parties like Democratic Left and the Progressive Democrats have wielded the reins of power in administrations with the three long-established parties, Fianna Fáil, Fine Gael and Labour. Prior to 1987, such a situation could only be found almost five decades earlier, with the foundation of Clann na Poblachta in 1946.

The Clann, Family of the Republic, became home for republicans disillusioned with Fianna Fáil's approach to partition as well as those born after the Civil War who wanted to move on from the past and tackle the country's socio-economic problems. For a few years, from the end of the Second World War until the start of the 1950s, Clann na Poblachta upset the Irish political establishment. The party was driven by men like Seán MacBride and Dr Noël Browne. It threatened Fianna Fáil's stranglehold on power.

The policies Clann pursued while part of the country's first multi-party government meant that the party's influence was felt for many years after the first inter-party administration split following the Mother and Child controversy.

This book traces the story of Clann na Poblachta from its foundation in 1946 through its involvement in government to the years of decline until its eventual end in 1965. This is not an academic work but an attempt to tell the story of a political party which sought to break the established framework within which Irish politics operated – and, for a time, succeeded.

1

1946: THE PARTY BEGINS

Irish political life changed totally when Fianna Fáil won power for the first time in 1932. Having come in from the political cold a number of years previously, the party, which had initially refused to sit in parliament, went on to wrest power from the pro-Treaty Cumann na nGaedheal. Over the following sixteen years Éamon de Valera came to dominate the political landscape. The other political parties were to find it almost impossible to challenge Fianna Fáil's near-institutional hold on power. De Valera's party was elected with a mandate to move away from the policies pursued over the previous decade by Cumann na nGaedheal. Fianna Fáil held strong views on removing the remaining links with Great Britain. It also proposed distinctive policies aimed at increasing economic growth and creating employment.

De Valera was not long Taoiseach when he set about implementing the Fianna Fáil agenda. The oath of allegiance to the British monarch hitherto taken by Oireachtas members was abolished. In addition, the role of the British representative, the Governor-General, was totally marginalised prior to the abolition of the position. This process was to culminate with the adoption of a new constitution in 1937, a constitution which to a significant extent embodied de Valera's political and social philosophy.

As well as attempting to eliminate all traces of British presence from the country, the Fianna Fáil government embarked on an economic policy aimed at providing the maximum possible level of self-sufficiency for agriculture and industry. The new administration argued that self-sufficiency was the only way of attaining the economic performance necessary to create jobs and increase general public welfare. Industrial policy was based on the introduction of protectionist measures, such as tariffs and quotas, on imports. These measures were intended to provide Irish industry with the space to expand and supply the domestic market, free from the threat of foreign competition. This same ethos of self-sufficiency dominated agricultural policy. Indeed, the expansion of agriculture was central to Fianna Fáil's economic policy. The party hoped to keep as many people as possible gainfully employed on the land.

However, the new government's economic policy was complicated by the dispute with the British authorities over the repayment of land annuities owed to the United Kingdom. These annuities were due for loans advanced by the British under the Land Acts of the previous fifty years. Irish tenants had bought out their holdings from their landlords using these monies. De Valera's government stopped the payment of these annuities. In response to this action, the British imposed levies on Irish cattle exports to recover the value of the annuities. The following years saw retaliation and counter-retaliation until compromise was finally reached in 1938.

While the Fianna Fáil government could claim considerable achievement for its constitutional and political policies during the 1930s, the same could not be said of its economic policies. The 'economic war' with Britain caused considerable damage to the Irish economy, while the self-sufficiency drives in agriculture and industry were only partially successful. Indeed, the country's failure to become economically self-sufficient was clearly highlighted during the war years when it was nearly impossible to obtain supplies of most basic necessities and essential raw materials.

With the onset of war in Europe in 1939, the government declared an 'Emergency'. Seán Lemass was put in charge of a newly established Department of Supplies, which was given responsibility for dealing with emerging shortages of key goods. During these years supplies of many products were seriously reduced. Sugar and tea were among the first items to disappear from shop shelves. Tea was rationed initially to two ounces per week for every person. However, as supplies became scarcer that amount was again cut by half. The most serious food shortages related to wheat. This prompted Éamon de Valera's government to introduce compulsory tillage, a policy which did not succeed in solving the problem.

Imports of coal, fertiliser and oil were also badly affected. The scarcity of fuel led to restrictions in transport services. Indeed, the trams in Dublin were suspended during the summer months of 1944. In *Ireland in the War Years and After*

James Meehan observes that four years into the Emergency, the country '... had twenty per cent of its normal requirements of tea, twenty per cent of its requirements of petrol, less than fifteen per cent of its paraffin, sixteen per cent of its gas coal, no domestic coal whatever and twenty-two per cent of its textiles.'

All in all, these were bleak years with widespread hardship. Indeed, people were being hit on all sides. Basic foodstuffs were in short supply and subject to rising prices. At the same time those in jobs were forced to accept wage restrictions. Over the war years, industrial production fell by almost 30 per cent and employment in industry declined by about 15 per cent. With such steep falls in production and employment, that constant feature of Irish life, emigration, became even more marked. It is estimated that between 1936 and 1946 about 18,700 people left the country every year.

In October 1945, the following analysis of the Irish economy appeared:

> This is a small country. It has a small population
> which is still dwindling, and limited national
> resources. The age constitution of the popul-
> ation is bad and is growing worse. Our economy
> is mainly agricultural and at that consists
> chiefly of small farms. Our economic position
> was relatively stagnant for a long period before
> the war. It has not since improved.

What was particularly damning about these comments was

that they were penned in the Department of Finance itself.

The ending of the war in Europe in 1945 did not bring any great improvement in Irish living standards. Many shortages continued for a further two years, some even as late as 1949. The bleak economic situation was not helped by the poor weather of 1946. The summer of that year remains one of the wettest on record. The wheat harvest was hit to such an extent that bread rationing had to be introduced for a time. To make matters worse the wet summer was followed by one of the coldest winters this century. In such a situation, public discontent increased in urban and rural areas. It was this unhappiness which the founders of Clann na Poblachta believed they could tap as a source of support.

In fact the first signs of electoral discontent had become evident in the 1945 presidential election. This was the first contested election for the office of president, which had been established under the 1937 constitution. Douglas Hyde had assumed office in 1938 with the agreement of all political parties. It was only in 1945 that the electorate were asked to decide who they wished to see occupying the position. They were presented with a choice of three candidates. Fianna Fáil nominated the Tánaiste, Seán T. O'Kelly. He came from a distinguished republican background, having been a founder member both of Sinn Féin and of the Irish Volunteers. He became Vice-President of Fianna Fáil when that party was founded in 1926 and successfully stood for election for the Dáil, first for Dublin North and then later for Dublin North-East. Having served as Minister for Local Government and Minister for Health, O'Kelly was appointed Minister for Finance in 1939. In the *Round Table* publications at the time of the election it was written of O'Kelly that 'in politics he has consistently, and quite efficiently, played the part of Sancho Panza to Mr de Valera's Don Quixote'.

The Fine Gael candidate was also a veteran of the independence movement. General Seán MacEoin, however, had sided with the pro-Treaty side. Indeed, he seconded the Dáil motion which approved the Treaty. A Dáil deputy since 1929, MacEoin represented the Longford-Westmeath constituency and had been closely associated with the Blueshirt movement in the 1930s.

The candidates of the two main parties were challenged by an Independent, Patrick McCartan, who shared their republican background. He was described as 'a medical man turned farmer' and had left public life in disgust at the outcome of the Treaty negotiations. McCartan was a last-minute nomination. He received the support of the other political parties, Labour and Clann na Talmhan, the farmers' party, as well as some Independents. Republicans unhappy with Fianna Fáil's position on the 'national question' also backed McCartan.

O'Kelly was the undoubted favourite, with observers predicting that he would win by a clear majority. Fianna Fáil, after all, was the only party really organised on a national level for the 1945 presidential election. The Fine Gael electoral machine was in disarray, while McCartan had the backing of a motley crew of supporters that lacked any sort of formal structure. In addition, Fianna Fáil used the campaign to tell the electorate that anything less than an overwhelming victory for O'Kelly would weaken the government. Éamon de Valera made clear his wish that the president chosen by the electorate should be a person with whom 'there would be no friction, no time lost in settling up difficulties that should not have arisen'. This person was clearly Seán O'Kelly.

When the first-count results were announced the Fianna Fáil candidate had narrowly failed to secure an overall majority on first-preference votes. O'Kelly received 537,965 first-preference votes while the Fine Gael candidate, MacEoin, had 335,539. Surprisingly, the outsider, McCartan, polled very respectably with 212,834 first preferences.

O'Kelly had won 49.5 per cent of the first preference vote and was only some 5,205 votes from outright victory. While there was a degree of concern in Fianna Fáil circles about the 20 per cent of the vote that McCartan had received, there was shock when his transfers were distributed. Just over 55 per cent of McCartan's transfers (117,886) went to the Fine Gael candidate and only 12.8 per cent (27,200) went to O'Kelly. While the transfers were enough for O'Kelly to secure victory, McCartan's performance and the strength of the anti-Fianna Fáil transfers were worrying for the government party. This was especially so given that McCartan, who went on to join Clann na Poblachta, achieved his result in 1945 without proper organisation and after only a few weeks of campaigning. There was obviously a large and growing sector of the electorate that was dissatisfied with de Valera's party. Some took this as indicating the potential for a third party alternative to Fianna Fáil and Fine Gael.

In the mid-1940s it was apparent that any challenge to Fianna Fáil's dominance was unlikely to come from the established parties, which were undergoing periods of change. Fine Gael was totally demoralised. The party's historian Brian Maye claims that Fianna Fáil's electoral victory at the 1937 general election 'ushered in for Fine Gael the eleven most dismal and disastrous years in the history of the party'. Even at subsequent elections, when Fianna Fáil's popularity began to wane, Fine Gael was unable to take advantage. In the June 1943 general election, in which all other groups made ground on Fianna Fáil, Fine Gael lost thirteen seats, including those of two former ministers. One of these, Richard Mulcahy, went on to succeed W. T. Cosgrave as party leader in early 1944. In the general election of that year, Fine Gael could muster only fifty-seven candidates, which was not enough to win an overall majority even if all were to be elected. The party was bedevilled by financial difficulties. Of the ten by-elections between 1944 and 1948 it contested only six, losing them all.

The advent of Clann na Talmhan was one source of Fine Gael troubles. Formed by Michael Donnellan in 1938 to represent the interests of small western farmers, the party took votes from both Fianna Fáil and Fine Gael. In the 1943 general election Clann na Talmhan won ten seats, returning one TD less in the general election of the following year. Joseph Blowick from Castlebar in Mayo took over as leader in 1944 and was to serve in both inter-party governments. However, Clann na Talmhan could never hope to win power on its own. It was always going to be a niche party representing a distinct sectional interest group.

Any possibility of Labour Party growth on the back of disillusionment with Fianna Fáil and turmoil within Fine Gael evaporated after a bitter internal dispute which came to a head in 1944. The divisions were a combination of personality clashes, trade union fighting and left-right ideological conflict. This row eventually resulted in the secession of five of Labour's Dáil deputies. They went on to set up their own grouping called National Labour.

Much but not all of the discontent with Fianna Fáil stemmed from the poor economic situation. Fianna Fáil had been brought to power in 1932 with the support of the IRA. On taking office the new government sought to repay that support. IRA prisoners were released, the ban on the *An Phoblacht* newspaper was lifted and the outlawing of the IRA as an organisation was revoked. In addition, the Military Tribunal, which had been established by the previous government to deal with those who did not give the new state their full democratic support, was suspended.

But the honeymoon between the Fianna Fáil government and the IRA did not last. Even though the government attracted many people away from the IRA, with the offer of state pensions for veterans of the Civil War, the organisation continued to refuse to enter constitutional politics. Its return to violence in the late 1930s led to further distance between the republican movement and Éamon de

Valera. Eventually the Fianna Fáil government began to act with vigour and ruthless determination against former comrades in the republican movement. This policy intensified during the Emergency years when internment was widely used. Six IRA men were executed and three veterans of the republican struggle were allowed to die on hunger strike.

Many supporters of the republican cause had become unhappy with Fianna Fáil's performance and what they saw as its 'tacit acceptance' of partition. The proscription of the IRA and the use of emergency powers against it, instead of an attempt to reach some form of accommodation, further distanced many republican supporters. Ironically the man in charge of the Department of Justice during this time was Gerry Boland, who had been interned by the British for his part in the 1916 Rising. Boland had been active in the IRA during the War of Independence and the Civil War. His brother Harry had been killed by Free State soldiers while trying to escape from imprisonment in 1922.

Despite this republican background, Gerry Boland adopted a no-nonsense and ruthless approach to those who still advocated the gun in Irish politics. There was no political status for republican prisoners, a policy that led to several IRA men going on hunger strike. The hunger strike had been used by several republicans as a form of passive resistance in the final years of British rule in Ireland. In 1917 Thomas Ashe, who had taken part in the 1916 Rising and was a former President of the Irish Republican Brotherhood, went on hunger strike after refusing to work or to wear prison clothes. He died in Mountjoy Prison after being force-fed in an attempt to end his hunger strike.

In 1920 Terence MacSwiney, who had been elected Mayor of Cork in March of the same year, died in an English prison after a seventy-three-day fast. It was ironic that supporters of Ashe and MacSwiney were among those who adopted an intransigent policy as former colleagues embarked on similar forms of resistance. In 1939 Patrick McGrath, a veteran of the 1916 Rising, was one of the first IRA men to go on hunger strike. His condition deteriorated quickly but the public outcry forced the government to release him after a twenty-three-day fast.

The Fianna Fáil government was, however, determined to break the IRA. It did not give in on the next occasion IRA men in prison used hunger strikes as a weapon. In April 1940 the government refused to release from Mountjoy Prison Tony D'Arcy and Jack McNella, who had gone on hunger strike. When the hunger strikers died, government censors restricted press coverage in order to limit any public outcry about their deaths. At the time newspapers reported Éamon de Valera as saying: 'the government have been faced with the alternative of two evils. We have had to choose the lesser, and the lesser is to let men die rather than the safety of the whole community be threatened.' In 1946, Seán McCaughey, who was the IRA's Chief of Staff when he was arrested, went on hunger strike for political status. He died after refusing water as well as food in his final days. Ironically the inquest into McCaughey's death was to bring a young barrister, Seán MacBride, to the public's attention.

Throughout these years there was much discussion in the

republican movement as to the future direction it should take. There was strong opposition within the IRA to the formation of a political party to articulate its views. However, many of those involved in setting up Clann na Poblachta were former IRA men, who were prepared to try constitutional politics as a means of achieving their objectives.

There had been a number of previous attempts at forming a political party to represent the republican constituency which felt alienated from Fianna Fáil. Córas na Poblachta had been formed on the back of protests at the execution of two IRA members in England. It nominated five candidates in the 1943 general election, all of whom lost their deposits. The party did not show its head again.

One of those favouring the establishment of a new political party to represent such a constituency was Seán MacBride, who in the mid-1930s had been Chief-of-Staff of the IRA. Seán MacBride was born in Paris in January 1904. His father, John MacBride, had been executed for his part in the 1916 Rising. His mother was Maud Gonne MacBride, who was herself involved in the republican movement. Family friends considered his birth of national significance, sending telegrams of congratulations some of which referred to the birth of the 'future president of Ireland'. Maud Gonne's biographer, Margaret Ward, refers to one family friend sending a telegram to the Pope announcing that 'the King of Ireland has been born'.

As a young boy Seán MacBride spent much time in Paris, where he acquired a pronounced French accent which remained with him for the rest of his life. He studied at

University College Dublin and later at the King's Inns. While in his teens, he was actively involved in the republican struggle. He joined the IRA in 1919 and became a member of Michael Collins's staff. He was part of the Irish entourage which travelled to London to negotiate the Treaty. He was given responsibility for carrying messages and information across the Irish Sea between London and Dublin. Despite his closeness to Collins, MacBride supported the anti-Treaty side during the Civil War. By 1927 he held the position of Director of Intelligence in the IRA.

In 1936, at a juncture when the IRA was divided on the subject of the future direction it should take, Seán MacBride was Chief of Staff. A year later he left the IRA. He later said that the 1937 constitution had been sufficient for him to turn his back on physical force and observed that Clann na Poblachta 'was started because of the realisation that physical force by itself really could not succeed'. While there may be a degree of truth in this, MacBride was in fact always on the political wing of the IRA. Indeed, there was a degree of hostility towards him by the more militant sections of the organisation. When he left the IRA, MacBride initially earned his living as a journalist while beginning a new career as a barrister. He was called to the bar in 1937 and became a senior counsel in 1942. He maintained his links with the republican movement as many of his clients were members of the IRA.

Seán MacBride was a well known figure. Prior to the formation of Clann na Poblachta, he had been in the public eye at the inquest into the death of IRA man, Seán

McCaughey, who died while on hunger strike in Portlaoise Prison. MacBride acted as senior counsel for the relatives at the inquest. His junior counsel at the inquest was a future Clann na Poblachta colleague, Noel Hartnett, while another future Clann member, Con Lehane, was also involved. MacBride succeed in gaining publicity for the poor conditions the IRA man had endured prior to his death. McCaughey's cell was underground and has been described as a truly awful place. As the inquest was concluding with the prison doctor giving evidence, MacBride asked 'You would not keep a dog in conditions like that, would you, Doctor?' Initially the doctor declined to answer but MacBride persisted with his question until the doctor agreed with him.

After they turned their back on militant republicanism MacBride and many others like him found that Fianna Fáil, as a republican party, offered them little. They were unhappy with the treatment of political prisoners and disillusioned with Fianna Fáil's economic policies. There was an increasing sense that a republican-based party was a real possibility. This eventually led to the formation of Clann na Poblachta by a small group of republicans, many of whom had spent the war years interned in the Curragh.

Among those involved in the formation were Con Lehane, Noel Hartnett, Dr Richard Batterberry and Fionán Breathnach. These men met in Lehane's rooms on Ormonde Quay in Dublin. Lehane had been a member of the IRA Army Council in the 1930s but had parted with the IRA in 1938 when it decided on a bombing campaign in England. He had been jailed for eighteen months in 1935 by the Military

Tribunal which had been established by de Valera's government. He was also briefly interned in 1939 under the Offences Against the State Act.

It is understood that MacBride had proposed The O'Rahilly Junior as leader but it can never have been in any doubt that MacBride would himself lead the new party. He was the dominant figure, the one who would attract national attention and public respect. The party was inaugurated in Barry's Hotel in Dublin on Saturday 6 July 1946 and given the name Clann na Poblachta, which translates as Family or People of the Republic. Its emergence was to give new impetus to the belief in the possibility of an alternative government to Fianna Fáil.

In an unpublished thesis, P. D. O'Keeffe has noted that 'at least twenty-two out of a total of twenty-seven of the Provisional Executive of Clann na Poblachta were active in the IRA at some stage in their lives'. One member, Michael Ferguson, had been released from prison only the previous March. He had been active in the 1939 IRA bombing campaign in England. Another member of the Provisional Executive, Simon Donnelly, was reported as having been a spokesperson for the Old IRA. On the morning after the announcement of the formation of Clann, *The Irish Times* quoted 'a prominent member of the committee' as stating that the new party meant that a significant number of 'what you might call the IRA' were taking constitutional action.

The membership of the Provisional Executive may have given the impression that Clann was another republican party following on from the disaster that was Córas na

Poblachta. Those involved in setting up the new party were fully aware that to be successful it was vital that Clann was more than a republican party even if republicanism were to be its dominant characteristic. The first statement of the Provisional Executive attempted to achieve this purpose by referring to standards in political life and the need for greater radicalism in economic affairs. Those involved claimed that they wanted to set 'a new standard of political morality in public life'. This was to be achieved by 'a truly independent and distinctive national organisation'.

The initial statement of the founding members stated that their intention was to leave the formulation of a detailed policy programme and a constitution until the new party held its first Árd Fheis. The statement did, however, clearly set down the reasons why Clann na Poblachta was being formed. It also gave some idea of the areas on which the party would focus its attention:

> For many years a large section of republican opinion has felt that republicans should take an active part in the political life of the Nation. It was felt that it would be possible to work for the achievement of republican ideals by purely political means. It was felt that the cycles of repression and violence which marked the history of the last quarter of a century could provide no solution and could weaken the national effort. Various causes combined to prevent political development. Not least of

these was the low standard of political morality
set by those who in the name of republicanism
secured office. The continual inroads on element-
ary personal rights (quite apart from Emergency
legislation) also rendered it difficult to instil in
republicans confidence in political action.

The initial statement also indicated the intention of the new
party to go beyond the republican label and rise above what
Trinity College Dublin political scientist, Michael Gallagher,
has called the 'limited appeal of extreme republicanism'.
Emphasis was also placed on improving people's welfare and
material living standards. It was Clann's policies in such
areas that subsequently attracted the likes of Noël Browne
and Jack McQuillan into the party. Both were later Dáil
deputies for Clann and were to be involved in the turmoil
when it went out of office.

The statement took a swipe at the perceived inaction of
Fianna Fáil in government:

The nation is being weakened by the forced
emigration of its youth. A small section has
been enabled to accumulate enormous wealth
while unemployment and low wages, coupled
with an increased cost of living, are the lot of
the workers.

The justification for the new party included the need to
tackle these issues:

> It has been apparent that if these evils, and the system responsible for them, are to be ended there must arise a strong political party that will set up an ideal before the nation and a new standard of political morality in public life. Democratic institutions can only survive if they can command the respect and confidence of the people as a whole. A Nation without an ideal is like a body without a soul. A country without strong public opinion is like a man without a conscience.

The new party proposed to organise branches throughout the country so as to be in a position to contest elections and enter the Dáil. The Provisional Executive was vested with the authority to run Clann until its first Árd Fheis was held. The twenty-seven members of the Provisional Executive were all resident in Dublin but the initial statement made clear that this situation would be rectified at the party's Árd Fheis. The policies later put forward by Clann convinced many people that the new party had the solutions to the problems which bedevilled the country. It is interesting to note that one of the party's early pamphlets, 'You and the Future', made absolutely no reference to partition or anything to do with republican ambitions but concentrated on other Clann policies such as social insurance, price controls and the need for national planning of the country's economic affairs.

Clann na Poblachta attracted people who had been active

in the other parties, some of whom went on to become Clann candidates in the 1948 general election. In addition, the new party sought to attract those who found the other main parties unreceptive to new blood and fresh ideas. Fianna Fáil's leadership was ageing; new men and women were not progressing up the ranks. There was a low turnover of members of the Oireachtas. Clann presented itself as representing, among other things, a forum for this excluded generation. Its early literature played on this issue. One of its first leaflets noted: 'You may have taken an active interest in public affairs, or you may not. You may have been too young, or too disenchanted. But be that as it may, this is addressed to you, whether you had any previous political views or not'.

Clann's early statements also demanded an end to what it called 'political corruption, quibbling, jobbery and graft'. The party argued that corruption had become the trademark of Fianna Fáil in power. Timing is all-important in politics, and in July 1946, as Clann was being established, fortune smiled when a Fianna Fáil Parliamentary Secretary was forced to resign.

Dr Francis Ward had been Parliamentary Secretary at the Department of Local Government and Public Health since 1932, when Fianna Fáil first entered government. He was also the owner of a bacon factory in County Monaghan. The brother of a man who had been dismissed from the factory wrote to the Taoiseach making a number of allegations of corruption against Dr Ward. A Tribunal of Enquiry was set up in June 1946 and reported in early July. The report of the tribunal found Dr Ward innocent of most of the charges made against him but concluded that Dr Ward had been guilty of making incomplete returns to the revenue commissioners in relation to the bacon factory. These irregularities forced Dr Ward to resign his government position within a week of the publication of the report. It is ironic to note that Ward had been heavily involved in negotiations with the medical profession and the Catholic hierarchy about the terms of what was to become the 1947 Public Health Act.

It has been observed that one of the characteristics of the emergence of Clann in Irish political life was the number of teachers who became members. George Lawlor joined Clann not long after it was founded. He came from a republican background and was soon in charge of the area near his Mespil Road home. He recalls jokingly that 'nearly everyone who joined was a teacher. They brought ideas to the party because they were educated.'

The teachers' strike of March to October 1946 brought an influx of teachers into Clann, as the new party supported their cause. P. D. O'Keeffe has noted that 'four out of a total of eleven on the INTO strike administrative committee were actively associated with Clann'. National teachers were unhappy with the way their salary scales were determined. At that time, inspectors of the Department of Education classified teachers under three headings – 'highly efficient', 'efficient' or 'non-efficient'. Around a third of teachers were placed in the 'highly efficient' category. This brought a higher salary than teachers in the other two categories. However, it was believed this rating system was open to abuse. Teachers rejected proposals resulting from salary negotiations between the INTO and the government at the beginning of 1946. A bitter eight-month strike of teachers in schools throughout Dublin was the result. Preaching a message different from Fianna Fáil's, the new party made itself attractive to many in the teaching profession.

Dissatisfaction with the economic situation and the problem of spiralling prices attracted many people to Clann because the party appeared to be offering an alternative to Fianna Fáil's policies. The prices and supplies issue led to the establishment of a Women's Parliament. Three hundred thousand women from all parts of the country participated. Clann na Poblachta was listed as one of the organisations involved in this group and two of the six demands of the Parliament were also Clann policy. A political party formed to contest the 1944 general election, *Ailtirí na hAiseirghe* (translated as Architects of Resurrection), also supplied members and supporters to Clann. That party performed very poorly in the 1944 general election but this failure was to benefit Clann.

As well as determining its policy agenda, to become a national party Clann had to establish an organisational base and structures throughout the various consitituencies. If this was not done it faced the possibility of becoming a niche party, like Clann na Talmhan. The organisational structure of the new party was based on the Fianna Fáil model, which was itself modelled on the 1922 Sinn Féin structure. Party documents stated that until they were ratified at its first Árd Fheis, the initial rules were of a provisional nature. Membership was open to 'every Irish citizen'. The unit of organisation was known as the 'craobh' (branch). The original affiliation fee for each craobh was set at ten shillings. The craobh was allowed to raise this affiliation fee by applying a membership subscription. Each craobh elected a chairman, treasurer and secretary. In addition, other officers could be elected as 'deemed necessary to provide an efficient working unit'.

The Provisional Executive held the authority to establish 'a comhairle ceanntair [regional committee] in any area in which at least five craobhacha have been registered'. The comhairle ceanntair was to consist of two delegates from each registered craobh in the area. Each craobh and each comhairle ceanntair was obliged to meet on a monthly basis. The intention was that the first Árd Fheis would be held as soon as a sufficient number of craobhacha were registered. That Árd Fheis was to formulate the rules and constitution of the party and elect its trustees, officers and the ard-chomhairle (executive committee) of the organisation. The party's Provisional Executive remained in place until Clann's first Árd Fheis was eventually held at the end of November 1947.

2

POLICIES NOT PERSONALITIES

The political climate in the late 1940s was ideal for the creation of a new force in Irish politics. After a decade-and-a-half of rule by one party the electorate was discontented with low living standards, not to mention the ever-present spectre of emigration. Clann leaflets summed up the reasons for the country's depressed economic situation in a number of brief sentences. 'The greater the emigration the fewer the people are left to work, the fewer the people work the smaller becomes national productivity and the smaller becomes the purchasing power of the people. Shortage of goods and increased cost of living are the inevitable results.'

Clann policy aimed to remedy this situation and win supporters in the process. A number of different policy areas were identified in party leaflets and pamphlets published throughout 1947. These publications carried headings such as 'Full Employment', 'Social Security', 'Rural Life', 'Education' and 'Finance'. Clann policy was very much influenced by Seán MacBride and his group of friends and advisers. Indeed afforestation and the retrieval of sterling assets were two favourites of the party's leader.

Some of the ideas and language used in Clann publications were influenced by Catholic social teaching. As one leaflet put it:

> The structure of the Christian state is based on the family. Sociologically and morally family life is essential to the nation. Likewise, the economic organisation must be based on the family unit. There can be no social security unless each family unit can provide for its members a reasonable standard of living in terms of modern requirements.

Clann propounded a policy which, the party's founding members argued, would achieve full employment. This policy was to be combined with a basic minimum wage based on the cost of living. In many cases Clann resisted the temptation to attack Éamon de Valera's government directly. Instead it laced the language in its publications with subtle criticisms of the country's economic situation, highlighting the need to provide 'work at good wages instead of emigration, doles and unemployment'.

The new party believed that the state should assume 'responsibility for the employment of those who are un-employed'. These people would be employed by the state on 'afforestation, housing, hydro-electrification and other con-structional works of national or social importance'. A comprehensive social insurance would assist 'those incapacit-ated for work through old age, illness or family duties'.

These people would receive benefits based on the basic minimum wage. Clann literature stressed that this social insurance scheme would not turn out to be 'doles'. The party said the insurance would bring people 'security during sickness and old age'. As a part of this welfare provision 'housing, hospital and sanatorium accommodation' would be provided 'before luxury buildings'.

Clann espoused national planning as the means of attaining its economic policies, especially where the large-scale investment required would not be forthcoming from the private sector. The party proposed a massive range of state interventions in the economy to generate jobs. The housing problems in urban areas would be tackled with 'the demolition of slums and the provision of adequate housing' with each new house containing a kitchen and bathroom. The electrification of all rail transport was proposed. In addition, Clann wanted to develop the country's natural resources such as forestry and fishing. It suggested the creation of large inshore and deep-sea fishing fleets. The mining industry was to be targeted – coal and other minerals were mentioned – while bogs and turf by-products were also seen as a source of wealth. There would be spin-offs from these sectors. In the case of fishing, Clann saw industries producing by-products such as fish oils and fats. On top of all this, the Clann agenda for state intervention proposed the reclamation and drainage of land throughout the country.

One of the consequences of the Emergency was a substantial increase in Irish external reserves, held mostly in sterling. At the end of 1939, the net external assets held by

Irish banks amounted to £65.4 million; by 1944 they had doubled to £130.9 million. This reflected the artificial constraints imposed on Irish imports by the war. Most of the money earned from exports was not spent on imports but deposited in British banks or invested in British securities. Seán MacBride and his colleagues wanted to use this money to fund the development of forestry and education.

To achieve the latter objective, Clann proposed the establishment of a National Monetary Authority. The functions of this body would have been to 'equate currency and credit to the economic needs of full employment and full production'. The authority would also be vested with responsibility to provide 'credits free of interest for full employment and national development of industry and agriculture'. The views expressed by Clann were noted by officials in the Department of Finance with a degree of caution but at this stage Clann was still a new party without any elected representatives.

Afforestation was one of the policies which MacBride believed was central to any economic advancement. It was put forward as part of Clann policy for achieving full employment. Leaflets were produced to show how much potential was 'under-exploited' in this area. A comparison was drawn with Sweden which, Clann said, employed 150,000 in forestry work alone while 'seventy-five paper and cardboard mills employ 15,000; twenty-two distilling plants produce seventeen million kilogram of ethyl alcohol; sawmills, joinery and furniture works employ 53,500; the wood pulp industry employs 16,400'. Clann made the case that a spruce tree took 100–120 years to mature in Sweden, while in Ireland better weather conditions reduced that time to forty years. The party wanted to grow trees on the two million acres of non-arable land which it claimed was suitable for afforestation. The timber would then have a whole range of uses including housing, fuel, the production of wood pulp, paper, plastics, artificial silk, alcohol and motor fuel.

Clann's agricultural policies were not that far removed from those articulated by Fianna Fáil. However, as an opposition party, Clann had the advantage of pointing out the areas in which Fianna Fáil had not made use of being in power to translate its objectives into government policy. Leaflets supporting the Clann cause boldly stated: 'Nothing must be spared that can improve the conditions of those who work on the land, so as to make rural life more attractive to the young people.' It said its policy was to provide 'co-operative organisations based on elevated parish councils with statutory powers for the purpose of providing agricultural machinery, co-operative marketing . . . ' It was Clann's hope that these councils would promote 'mutual assistance on a neighbourly basis' and lead to the construction of parish halls, libraries and sports fields throughout the country. Clann's policy also included a commitment to guarantee prices for agricultural products. In addition, fertilisers were to be provided free of charge 'to increase the fertility of the land'.

It should not be thought that Clann policy was all about economics. The party noted that 'under modern materialistic conditions it is essential that the moral fibre of the people should be safeguarded and rehabilitated'. There was a danger, according to Clann, that 'alien, artificial and unchristian concepts of life are being constantly pumped into and absorbed by our people'. The party framed cultural and educational policies to address this situation. These included proposals to establish a national theatre and film industry. It was envisaged that the latter would aim to provide films on a competitive basis for domestic and foreign markets. Many Clann leaflets were published in both Irish and English. The party policies included proposals to safeguard and extend the Gaeltacht areas. It was suggested that efforts to extend the use of Irish as a spoken language could be assisted with the production of films and books. In addition, Clann proposed setting up a council 'for the diffusion and encouragement of a knowledge of music and the arts, particularly in provincial towns and rural areas'.

Clann claimed that 'the well-being of the nation is dependent upon the industry and good citizenship and the ability of the people to avail of the resources which God by His Providence has placed at their disposal'. It aimed to achieve this objective through the educational system. Clann policy included raising the school-leaving age to sixteen and the provision of free secondary and university education. Continuous courses in agricultural, domestic and technical subjects would be provided free of charge under a Clann government. The party had accepted the need for the establishment of a Council of Education which would represent the churches, parents, teachers and the universities.

Given Clann's republican constituency it was obvious

that it would hold strong views on partition and the 'national question'. The party declared that its 'ultimate aim is the reintegration of the whole of Ireland as a republic, free from any external association, save as may be freely entered into by the nation'. However, Clann was blunt in framing its ambitions in relation to partition. 'One of the realities that has to be faced is that until we set up social services and an economic system that are at least as good as those offered to the people of the Six Counties by the British Labour government, no serious advance can be made towards the ending of partition'.

Clann claimed that its other policies in the political, economic and social areas would 'render the unification of the nation more readily achievable'. However, given its significant republican membership the party could not simply limit its policy on the north to such a long-term aspiration. It argued for one immediate step: that 'the Dáil should be opened to the elected parliamentary representatives of the people of the Six Counties and their co-operation should be invited'. The party wanted to use all 'propaganda and diplomatic means available to the government' to assist its objectives in relation to ending partition. Greater co-operation between workers' and other organisations on both sides of the border was to be encouraged.

Clann made a big play on the need to end what it called 'political decadence'. The party proposed making the use of political influence a penal offence. Throughout 1947, in the by-elections of that year and the general election of 1948, Clann constantly referred to the government's decision to increase the levels of pensions paid to ministers. There were also repeated attempts to contrast the pay and conditions of TDs and government ministers with those of the population in general. Party leaflets emphasised that TDs' annual salaries had increased from £360 in 1938 to £624 in 1947, 'free of income tax'. In 1946 'when everyone was suffering hardship, ministers' salaries were increased by £10 per week'. The party claimed that 'an old person, who has given fifty years of work to the nation - either as a worker or as a mother - will, if completely destitute, receive an old age pension of 12/6 a week at the age of 70'. It then asked 'Could you live on 12/6 per week? Can they?' The answer was provided: 'Of course not.' This was followed by the sting: 'there are no means tests for Ministers or Parliamentary Secretaries – *there are for the old people*'. The attack on government policy concluded with the remark: 'The degree of civilisation of a state is judged by the care it gives to its children, its old people and its sick - not by luxury buildings and the pensions it gives to its politicians'.

As well as developing policies, Clann had to establish a structured party organisation in time to contest the next general election. Putting the local framework in place was of little value without the personnel to breathe life into these structures. Clann had to get people actively involved and attending local constituency meetings. In the process, it had to identify potential candidates for the forthcoming general election. In fact, the organisational methods were similar to those adopted by Fianna Fáil when it was founded in 1926. At that stage, Seán Lemass and other leading people in that party travelled around the country to explain Fianna Fáil policy and enlist supporters.

Every member of the Clann executive was requested to write to colleagues throughout the country, especially well-known and respected republicans who were unhappy with Fianna Fáil's performance. Two members of the executive were given responsibility to travel to the constituencies in an attempt to get such sympathetic republicans to join the party. An example of one man who joined Clann in this way was Patrick Kinnane from Tipperary. He was a veteran of the War of Independence. In an RTÉ documentary some years later, his wife recalled her husband joining Clann. 'Some of the members of the party came down to see Paddy. He didn't give his consent at that time. Seán MacBride had to come himself then. And after that he didn't even consent . . . so it took another while before he decided'.

Although many of the founding members of the party were well known, few had experienced the cut and thrust associated with the work of political parties. For this experience Clann was heavily dependent on two men, Noel Hartnett and Peadar Cowan. Hartnett had been a member of the Fianna Fáil National Executive. However, in the years immediately after Fianna Fáil came to power he became disillusioned with the policies it was pursuing. At a National Executive meeting in 1937 it was reported that a wealthy businessman had donated £1,000 to Fianna Fáil. Hartnett felt that it was unethical to accept the donation and proposed that the money be returned. Éamon de Valera, who was chairing the meeting, replied with impatience: 'Mr

Hartnett, we must be practical.' Hartnett was not convinced and resigned from Fianna Fáil.

Noel Hartnett was widely known as the compère of *Question Time* on National Radio but he fell foul of the station's authorities. This was because of what *The Irish Times* described as 'a violent speech which he made at a political meeting comparing conditions under which Irish republican prisoners were detained to those in German concentration camps'. Like Seán MacBride, Hartnett was a deeply religious man. He had joined Clann na Poblachta in the hope of achieving a synthesis of republicanism, socialism and Christianity. A brilliant orator and criminal lawyer, he had worked with MacBride on a number of cases, especially defending IRA members.

While Hartnett had strong Fianna Fáil associations, Peadar Cowan's allegiances were originally with the Labour Party; he was a former director of organisation for that party. Cowan had served as a captain in the Free State army during the 1920s. Prior to joining Labour, he had been associated with left-wing republican groups. He had practical experience of running for election, having stood unsuccessfully for Labour in the Meath-Westmeath constituency on four separate occasions. Cowan's views were to the left of the Labour leadership. Coupled with his strong republican beliefs, these had caused his expulsion from Labour in 1945.

Cowan and Hartnett were central to Clann's efforts to put down roots in the various constituencies as well as identifying people to stand as candidates. Although the party was founded in mid–1946 it really only began to get itself established as a recognised political party the following year. Part of this process involved expanding its membership base and setting up party structures. One means of achieving these objectives was to hold public meetings at which well known figures like Seán MacBride would speak. Posters and notices in local papers were used to invite the public to attend.

One such meeting was held in February 1947 in the Town Hall in Dun Laoghaire. Hartnett and MacBride were among the speakers who addressed the meeting, which was well attended. They attacked government policy, emphasising high prices, the fuel situation, the number of industrial strikes and, interestingly, the need for greater attention to prevent tuberculosis. Hartnett, using his oratorical skills to the full, sarcastically described the government's 'masterly inactivity' in dealing with these issues. Seán MacBride outlined Clann policy but, as was to become the norm at Clann public meetings over the following year, he held back from laying the blame directly on Éamon de Valera. 'The time has come when political thought should cease to be the monopoly of a few people who have been associated with the movement for independence and the subsequent splits.'

The new party received a boost in March 1947 when a Fianna Fáil cumann in Ballymore in County Roscommon decided to leave the government party. Local newspapers reported the cumainn members asking Clann to send an organiser 'so that a strong organisation may be established'. The party's ambitions were increasing all the time. One member, Seán Feeney, told a meeting in Waterford that

Clann would contest every constituency at the following general election. At the end of 1947, Con Lehane claimed that the party had five hundred branches throughout the country.

A review of electoral constituencies required by the constitution to be held at twelve-yearly intervals was due, at the latest, by the end of 1949. Fianna Fáil had been less than enthusiastic about looking at the issue when it was raised in 1942. It was believed that any changes in the composition of constituencies were likely to increase the number of seats in Dublin. The capital city was under-represented, with one Dáil deputy for every 25,000 population compared with one for an average of 20,700 for the rest of the country. Historian Joe Lee has argued that Labour was 'poised to profit from working-class resentment at wages and prices policy'. For this reason Fianna Fáil decided in 1942 to leave well enough alone for the time being.

However, the outcome of the 1945 presidential elections provoked a degree of concern in Fianna Fáil circles. The formation of Clann na Poblachta added to a need to re-examine the constituencies with a clear eye on the next general election. Seán MacEntee, as Minister for Local Government, was instructed to look at difficult constituencies from Fianna Fáil's viewpoint, drawing conclusions from the combined total vote received by McCartan and Fine Gael's Seán MacEoin. The Electoral Amendment Bill was published in October 1947. In his *Ireland 1912-1985*, Joe Lee notes that 'the contents clearly reflect the concern with the rise of

Clann na Poblachta'. In 1935 the number of TDs had been reduced from 152 to 138. Despite the fact that in the intervening twelve years the population had fallen, the 1947 bill increased the number of deputies to 147. This was the highest number permitted under the constitution. In addition, the number of three-seat constituencies was increased from fifteen to twenty-two. This latter action, the *Irish Independent* claimed, 'inevitably loads the electoral dice in favour of the big party'. A number of constituencies such as Limerick, Clare and Mayo South, where Clann would have had hopes of winning seats, were reduced to four-seaters, while constituencies where Clann's appeal would not have been as strong, such as Longford and Kilkenny, gained seats.

There were three Dáil seats vacant in 1947 due to the deaths of three deputies. These were William O'Donnell, a Clann na Talmhan TD for Tipperary, and two Fianna Fáil members, Michael Morrissey from Waterford and Patrick Fogarty, who had represented the constituency of Dublin County. The by-elections could not have come at a worse time for the government party. The cost of living was spiralling while industrial unrest had brought the country literally to a standstill. A bus and tram strike continued throughout September and October while banking staff were also on strike. A Price Control Bill was published at the beginning of October with the promise of a Prices Commission to investigate prices and profits while a supplementary budget was introduced later in the month. On top of all this, political scandal was again in the headlines, giving credence to Clann claims that Fianna Fáil had cosy arrangements with the business sector.

The writs for the by-elections were moved in the Dáil at the beginning of October. Polling day was set for 29 October. This was to be the first electoral test for Clann na Poblachta. The new party contested all three constituencies. Each offered a different type of challenge. The constituency of Dublin County stretched from the borough of Dun Laoghaire to the north county rural base. It was a large constituency with a varied social make-up. Farmers in Dublin had been badly affected by the poor weather which lasted from August 1946 until the spring of 1947. Four candidates contested the Dublin by-election – from Labour, Fine Gael, Fianna Fáil and Clann. Tommy Mullins had been selected as Fianna Fáil's standard-bearer a number of days before the writ was moved in the Dáil. Mullins was the General Secretary of Fianna Fáil and was expected to hold on to the party's seat. Labour nominated Seán Dunne, who held the position of General Secretary of the Federation of Rural Workers. The Fine Gael runner was described by Liam Cosgrave as a 'very able young candidate' – to which an unnamed person was reported as whispering that Fine Gael had many very able young candidates but not enough voters.

Clann nominated their leader to contest the Dublin vacancy. The former IRA Chief of Staff had covered almost the full spectrum of political activity, from having been on the run from Free State forces not too many years previously. Now Seán MacBride was taking the first steps to challenge former republican associates, who had themselves taken the constitutional road when Fianna Fáil entered Dáil Éireann.

The county of Tipperary was divided into two separate administrative entities for local government purposes. From 1923, Tipperary North Riding and Tipperary South Riding were combined in a single seven-seat Dáil constituency. The 1947 boundary changes made Tipperary North and South into three-seaters. However, the 1947 by-election, caused by the death of the sitting Fianna Fáil deputy, was on the basis of the old constituency boundaries, as were the by-elections in Waterford and Dublin.

Five candidates were selected to contest the Tipperary by-election. Fianna Fáil's candidate Seán Hayes was a republican veteran of the independence struggle from the south of the county. He had held a Dáil seat from 1927 until the 1937 general election when he was beaten by a Labour Party candidate. Hayes again ran unsuccessfully in the 1943 general election. The Fine Gael candidate, Jeremiah Ryan, was also a former TD. He had supported the Treaty and was active on the side of the Free State in Tipperary during the Civil War. For these efforts he was rewarded with the rank of colonel. Based in Thurles, Ryan had been successfully elected at the 1937, 1938 and 1943 general elections. He did not run in 1944 so, as was the case for Seán Hayes, the 1947 by-election was for him an attempt at a political comeback. Labour put forward a trade union official from Thurles while the Clann na Talmhan candidate had the task of holding on to the seat the late William O'Donnell had won for the party in the 1943 general election.

Clann's candidate, Patrick Kinnane, was well known

throughout Tipperary because of his republican background. It was this republican involvement which had marked him out to Clann's organisers as a potential candidate for the party in Tipperary. Kinnane would also have been known for his active involvement in the GAA and the co-operative milk suppliers. The *Tipperary Star* noted that he had 'been an unselfish and sincere worker in the republican cause for a long number of years' and that it was 'generally recognised that he makes a strong candidate'. Kinnane was unanimously selected at a convention of the party in Thurles attended by eighty delegates. The *Tipperary Star* observed: 'His was the only name put forward and the selection was so quick that Mr Seán MacBride . . . stated that it was a unique event in Irish political history'. Some of the most prominent republicans in Tipperary backed Kinnane. On the other hand, his election agent had been active in Fine Gael before transferring his support to the Clann. During the campaign Kinnane repeatedly promised his audience that, if elected, he would give his time and ability as best he could to the service of the people and the country.

At a constituency convention presided over by the Minister for Lands, Seán Moylan, the widow of the late Deputy Michael Morrissey was chosen by Fianna Fáil to stand in the Waterford by-election but the selection aroused controversy and was rejected by the Fianna Fáil National Executive. The *Munster Express* noted that the decision to reject her nomination 'came as a surprise locally'. In her place the executive put forward John Ormonde, a national school teacher, who had supported the anti-Treaty side during the Civil War.

Clann's candidate was Seán Feeney, who had the decided disadvantage of being Dublin-based. Neither did he have a republican background. A teacher and former hurler, Feeney claimed that the politics of the previous two decades had been based on 'personalities, slogans and catch-cries rather than policy'. This was a theme which Clann speakers were to concentrate on, and would repeat time and time again over the coming months.

The party's posters called on the electorate to 'Help to lay the foundation of a New Ireland'. In all three constituencies Clann attempted to appeal to a wide range of voters. For example, speakers claimed that the party represented young people. Fianna Fáil's Seán Moylan was having none of that. He declared: 'I have often heard people claiming that Clann na Poblachta is the party of youth. Most of them whom I know are my contemporaries, and I cannot any longer be regarded as a youth.'

Seán MacEntee opened the Fianna Fáil campaign with a bitter attack on MacBride and Clann. He claimed it was merely 'the revived Saor Éire'. This was an ill-fated, left-leaning republican group formed by MacBride in 1931. Fianna Fáil policy was to make people doubtful about Clann's constitutional intentions. As he was the best known Clann member, MacBride was repeatedly the subject of attack. Fianna Fáil repeatedly claimed he had never left the IRA and had been pro-German during the Emergency. During the by-election campaigns MacEntee even questioned MacBride's views in a letter to *The Irish Times*, claiming that the Clann leader had 'manifested a singular lack of judgement, foresight and political sagacity' in his previous involvements. Throughout the campaigns, there were also allegations about Clann links with communism. This red scare was to intensify during the general election campaign.

Clann countered the Fianna Fáil attacks head-on. At a rally in Waterford on 17 October MacBride accused Seán MacEntee of reducing the 'campaign to the level of the gutter'. On the accusation that he had been pro-German during the war MacBride said: 'This is a lie, and Mr. MacEntee knows that it is untrue. I had no sympathy with authoritarian dictatorships of any kind, whether German or Russian. I was not associated throughout the course of the war with a political movement of any kind. At every possible opportunity, I endorsed the policy of neutrality.' The Clann leader also called on de Valera to condemn MacEntee's aggression. He rounded on Fianna Fáil, questioning their credentials for public life by referring to the 1938 decision to vote pensions for life for politicians. The Clann leader accused MacEntee of starting 'a campaign of innuendo' against him in an attempt to deflect attention from Clann's agenda of highlighting Fianna Fáil's mismanagement of the country. That Clann rally in Waterford was reportedly 'well attended'. The *Munster Express* noted that MacBride 'talks with much impressement [*sic*] and has the gift of carrying its audiences a long way with him in his arguments and opinions'.

Fianna Fáil was aware of the strength of dissatisfaction among the electorate. The allegations of sleaze and the poor economic situation were denting its support. The government party sought to rally the electorate by making the by-elections a confidence test in its ability to govern. Seán Lemass, speaking in Clonmel, and the Taoiseach in Waterford stressed that the by-elections were a test of the government's credibility. A defeat would result in a general election being called. The public was told that any alternative to a majority Fianna Fáil government would be instability. De Valera described coalitions as 'weak' and 'an oasis in a war-blasted desert'. He claimed virtue in Fianna Fáil's dominant position. 'We are a national government and consequently can resist the unreasonable demands of any section.' Fianna Fáil used all the resources at its disposal in its attempt to secure victory in the by-elections. For example, the *Irish Press* newspaper gave its full support to the government. Clann speakers in the three by-election constituencies were critical of the position adopted by the paper.

Only too aware that the economy was the main issue of concern for the public, the Fianna Fáil government made attempts to ease the economic situation in the country. In mid-October 1947 a supplementary budget was introduced which included flour, sugar, tea and bread. Wages and prices were to be held at the prevailing levels but to pay for these measures the prices of liquor and tobacco were increased. *The Irish Times* noted that the government had acted with a 'strange courage' by introducing a supplementary budget mid-way through the by-election campaigns.

Naturally the budget received less praise from the opposition parties than it did from the press. Clann accused the government of trying to win the by-elections by pretending to reduce the cost of living. A leaflet was printed claiming that Fianna Fáil had 'fooled the people so often they think they can fool them again. With Fianna Fáil, fooling the people has been brought to a fine art.' The leaflet was headed 'A Scandalous Business'. It focused on the dual nature of the budget, whereby increased taxes on some items were subsidising reduced taxes on others.

> The new budget reduces the cost of living for a family of four, man, wife and two children, by less than 2/1d. a week. The actual reduction is less than 6¼d. per person a week. If a father smokes ten cigarettes and drinks a pint a day he pays an additional tax of 2/11d. per week. The new budget, instead of reducing the cost of living, increases it for that family by more than 10d. a week. Every time a man and his wife go to the pictures they pay extra new taxation of ¼d. under the latest Fianna Fáil budget.

Throughout October, accusations and counter-accusations continued on a whole range of issues between Fianna Fáil and the other parties. The *Tipperary Star* was later to observe that 'scandal and allegations of scandal were driven home relentlessly, and at times the language reached a vulgarity Tipperary had not heard before'. Indeed, Clann strategists showed that they themselves were not above political manipulation. On the eve of polling a two-page advertisement was placed in the *Irish Times* which took statements made some years earlier by Fianna Fáil's Dublin candidate, Tommy Mullins.

> We find here mentioned the Irish Republican Army, the Cumann na mBan, Fianna Éireann, the Communist Party of Ireland, the Labour Defence League, the Soviet Union, Saor Éire and so on. I do not know where the President (W. T. Cosgrave, leader of Cumann na nGaedheal) got his interesting information with regard to the objects of these organisations or some of them. I happen to belong to four of them and I know more about them than the President or any member of the Cumann na nGaedheal Party . . .

Clann ran this quotation from Mullins under the headline 'Which Four?' As an answer to the red scare allegations and claims Clann had communist leanings, the party took another remark made by Mullins. In October 1931 he had declared that 'Russia, for the time being, being graded amongst the enemies of capitalism and imperialism, is the friend of Ireland.' In Clann notices in the Dublin newspapers this statement ran under the headline 'The Fianna Fáil Candidate! Russia!'

As well as campaigning in his own constituency, Seán MacBride travelled to towns in Waterford and Tipperary to seek support for Kinnane and Feeney. At a rally in Nenagh near the end of the campaign, MacBride set out the clear choice the electorate faced. If they were satisfied with existing conditions they would not vote for Clann but if they were not satisfied with the other parties, the Clann leader argued that they should vote then for his party as the only alternative. Peadar Cowan was another whom Clann used as a spokesperson in the three constituencies. Just before polling day he said the time had come for the electorate to choose better candidates instead of being 'voting machines who performed their parliamentary functions with their feet rather than with their brains'.

In all three constituencies, Clann was reported to have had an efficient election machine. According to the party's advertisements in local Tipperary newspapers, Directors of Elections were in place for north, south and mid-Tipperary. Indeed, one scribe wrote that 'the number of cars bearing the party's slogan surprised many' on polling day. The *Irish Independent* described Clann as being 'the best equipped party'. Despite the party's best efforts it was generally considered it would do well to put up a good show. This performance could then be built upon for later electoral contests. The polling day edition of *The Irish Times* predicted wins for Fianna Fáil in all three constituencies. In Tipperary it was forecast that Kinnane would weaken Fianna Fáil's vote but Clann's chance of snatching the seat from Fianna Fáil was considered too much to expect from the new party.

But Clann was to cause a political sensation. Seán MacBride and Patrick Kinnane won seats in Dublin County and Tipperary. The Clann candidates were elected with the help of transfers from the two main opposition parties. Over half of Labour's transfers went to Clann na Poblachta. At Labour rallies in Tipperary, party supporters had been urged to transfer votes to the Clann na Poblachta candidates and they did so to a large extent. The votes of the Labour Party's candidate had a massive influence on the eventual outcome. Kinnane got 3,277 Labour transfers compared to 1,712 for the Fianna Fáil candidate and 1,409 for Fine Gael. These votes were enough for the Clann candidate to beat Fine Gael into second place. Kinnane subsequently got 6,984 of Fine Gael transfers compared to 1,779 for Hayes; in other words, just under 48 per cent of Fine Gael's transfers passed to Clann, 15 per cent went to Fianna Fáil while the rest were non-transferable. It was not unexpected that the majority of Fine Gael's first preferences should be turned into anti-Fianna Fáil transfers but the proportion that went to Clann caused some surprise, given that Fine Gael and Clann appeared to be at opposite ends of the political spectrum.

While there were celebrations in Dublin and Tipperary, Clann was found to be totally exposed in Waterford, where the party was run into fourth and last place. It received a mere 8.5 per cent of the first-preference vote and John Ormonde took the seat for Fianna Fáil. Con Lehane blamed the Waterford defeat on lack of preparation in the constituency. The party had been active in Waterford for only two weeks prior to the by-election and had little organisation in place. It was a costly mistake to select a candidate without an established network of local contacts and a strong local base.

The Fianna Fáil cabinet met immediately to discuss the outcome of the by-elections. True to his word, Éamon de Valera announced that a general election would be held early in the new year, although no date was fixed. This general election was to be the seventh in just under sixteen years of Fianna Fáil rule. De Valera's justification for an election at this juncture was slim enough. Despite the by-election results, his government still had a majority of fourteen in the Dáil and there were two years to go before a general election had to be called. In fact Fianna Fáil had lost only one seat, in Dublin; it won in Waterford, while the Tipperary vacancy had been caused by the death of a Clann na Talmhan deputy.

The reality was that in calling an early general election de Valera was attempting to catch Clann before the party had an attempt to consolidate the by-election successes. The Fianna Fáil leader was aware of the appeal to the electorate of a party such as Clann na Poblachta. As his own party had done in 1932, Clann was offering something different from the established parties. The evidence from the three by-elections was that a significant proportion of the electorate was prepared to desert their traditional loyalty to Fianna Fáil and vote Clann na Poblachta.

An editorial in *The Irish Times* at this time noted that Clann had so far 'not had much chance to build up a nation-wide organisation, but it has made a surprisingly good start.' However, the newspaper was sceptical of Clann's ability to change society. 'Its policy . . . differs in few, if any essentials, from that of either Fianna Fáil or Fine Gael . . . {its} . . . only merit is the fact that it represents something new, although its declared policy is as old as Sinn Féin and its economic programme scarcely deserves to be taken seriously.' Despite Seán MacBride's commitment to constitutional politics for over a decade, *The Irish Times* was concerned that Clann was 'led by a man with a political record of uncompromising republicanism'. Regardless of the newspaper's doubts about Clann policies and its leader, it was asking the same questions which were no doubt taxing de Valera's mind: 'Will Fianna Fáil retain power? And if so with what majority? And if Fianna Fáil does not get a majority what party will be asked to form a government?'

The two Clann TDs took their Dáil seats on 5 November 1947. Seán MacBride sat behind the representatives of the farmers' party, Clann na Talmhan. According to the Irishman's Diary of *The Irish Times*, it would 'not be long, a cynical voice suggested in the press gallery, before they are taking up position behind him'. There was a round of applause from the opposition benches and public galleries. This was met by a 'shhhhhing from government benches'. Moreover, the Ceann Comhairle reminded the House of the impropriety of applause.

The Clann leader made his maiden speech later that same day. It was on a motion to set up a judicial inquiry to examine the circumstances surrounding the controversial sale of Locke's Distillery at Kilbeggan. He supported the need for an inquiry but addressed the issue in a broader context of the need to remove suspicion from the public's mind of too cosy a relationship between business and government.

Over the following weeks Seán MacBride raised in the Dáil a variety of issues connected with Clann policy. Subjects on which he made contributions and asked questions included government policy on the railways, India's opposition to admitting Ireland to membership of the United Nations, Irish membership of the International Monetary Fund, foreign trawlers fishing in Wexford Bay and the cost of living for an average Dublin family. On one occasion, having failed to elicit an adequate response from the Minister for Health, MacBride asked whether the Minister was 'aware that the failure to provide adequate sanatoria accommodation is tantamount to condemning a number of tuberculosis sufferers to death?'

Patrick Kinnane spoke on only one occasion before the dissolution of the Dáil for the general election. He put a parliamentary question concerning the closure of a branch railway line in his constituency. Indeed, throughout his Dáil career Kinnane's contributions were limited mainly to matters pertaining to his constituents in Tipperary.

The by-election successes gave Clann a massive boost and its presence in the Dáil gave it credibility. With a general election imminent it was vital that the party organise in the constituencies to consolidate the by-election gains. In addition, Clann's performance in Waterford had highlighted potential weaknesses in its structures. Despite having been eighteen months in existence, Clann was not yet ready for a general election. Increasingly, Noel Hartnett took over responsibility for organisational matters. His task was helped by the by-election victories. Membership now increased dramatically and units of the organisation were formed throughout the country.

The party had its headquarters at Herbert Place in Dublin. According to activist George Lawlor, Clann rented the entire basement and some rooms on the ground and first floors. Lawlor lived close by and was one of those with front door keys. He recalls that several beds were kept on the premises for members from outside Dublin who needed a place to stay after attending party meetings.

On 30 November, a year-and-a-half after its formation, Clann na Poblachta held its first Árd Fheis. *The Irish Times* reported that 372 delegates attended, reperesenting 252 constituency branches. These figures indicate that the party had an average of six branches in each constituency and confirm that Clann was in reality very poorly organised nationwide. Given this, it was not surprising the Árd Fheis decided that the new National Executive should have as much of a regional spread as possible to its membership. Of the eighteen members elected, fifteen represented the twenty-six counties while three came from the six counties of Northern Ireland. Only three of the eighteen members of the outgoing provisional executive lost their seats. The executive elected by the first Clann Árd Fheis to succeed the provisional body formed in 1946 had six new members. Only two of these members can be said not to have been from the republican wing of the party, so in reality the strong republican element of Clann was maintained.

The Árd Fheis adopted eight 'guiding fundamental principles', which were detailed in the party's newsletter in early December 1947. One of the resolutions unanimously passed by delegates stated: 'that this Árd Fheis emphatically repudiates the suggestions that Clann na Poblachta has communist, fascist or unconstitutional tendencies and declares that such whispered suggestions and innuendoes are merely devices utilised by the supporters of the Fianna Fáil party in an effort to maintain themselves in office.'

The Árd Fheis failed to address the challenges which Clann faced. Noël Browne now believes that it 'failed to establish a properly structured organisation, with clearly defined radical, social and economic policies. It merely emphasised the party's utopian woolliness and reflected MacBride's tenuous understanding of political, economic and philosophical problems.' Nevertheless, members were buoyed up by the party's by-election victories. With a general election expected sooner rather than later, Seán MacBride's mother, Maud Gonne wrote: ' . . . every young thing I know were working, talking and thinking of nothing but the elections, ever since the amazing and inexplicable rage of the government over Seán's being made a TD at the by-election . . . I never saw as much voluntary work given by young people since the early days of the Sinn Féin government.'

3

THE 1948 GENERAL ELECTION

The by-election campaigns in October 1947 turned out to be a dry run for the real thing. Because the Fianna Fáil government was committed to calling a general election, there was no let-up once the results of the by-elections became known. While the general election campaign began in earnest on 1 November, Éamon de Valera did not set the date of the election until mid-December. Frustrated members of the opposition parties repeatedly raised the issue in the Dáil. When the Labour Party leader, William Norton, tried to elicit information on the election date, all the Taoiseach would say was to advise him to 'look sharp'. Increasingly, however, the government acted as if on an election footing. Numerous measures were introduced to raise its popularity after the setbacks in the by-elections.

Strategically, the Fianna Fáil leader timed his move well. Just before Christmas 1947, 4 February 1948 was set as the date for the general election. Representatives of the national newspapers were summoned to Government Buildings, where they were told by the Taoiseach that: 'a government whose position has been weakened and might be questioned could not hope to deal effectively with the conditions which may confront the country in the coming year. An opportunity must be given to the people to indicate their will and to give their judgement. I think it is right, therefore, that I should seek a dissolution of the present Dáil as soon as practicable.'

Because of the by-election successes, there was confidence among Clann supporters when the general election was eventually called. Clann wanted to show that it was a party of government so it was vital for it to be seen to challenge Fianna Fáil's dominant position and de Valera's sixteen years of continuous power. For this reason, Clann nominated candidates in every constituency, ninety-three candidates in all. This was eleven more than Fine Gael, a party that was still in turmoil and disarray.

The general strategy was to run two candidates in three- and four-seater constituencies and three candidates in five-seaters, although there were a number of constituencies where these rules did not apply. For example, in Mayo North, a three-seat constituency, Clann nominated three candidates, while only one candidate was selected for the three-seat Cork South constituency. This electoral strategy appears to have been based on the somewhat naïve assumption that those voting for a particular Clann candidate would continue to vote the party ticket. In addition, it carried the risk that a significant number of Clann candidates would lose their deposits.

The majority of Clann candidates had been identified and selected only in the weeks prior to polling day. This was one of the areas in which the efforts of Clann's original members had fallen short. In some cases, Clann tried to attract up-and-coming young people. An indirect approach was made to future Fianna Fáil Taoiseach Jack Lynch to stand as a Clann candidate in Cork, but he declined.

Dr Noël Browne was asked to consider letting his name go forward for Clann by Noel Hartnett because of a mutual friendship with Harry Kennedy, an *Irish Times* journalist. Harry Kennedy was a patient at Newcastle Sanatorium where Browne worked and Noel Hartnett met Browne there while visiting Kennedy. It was Kennedy who suggested that the young doctor try politics as a means of bringing about improvements in the treatment of TB. Browne had been the first Secretary of the Irish TB Society and was one of the 'bright young things' whom Hartnett tried to get to stand for Clann. Colleagues of Harry Kennedy in *The Irish Times* later collected one hundred pounds to pay for him to go to London for treatment but he died while undergoing an operation.

In addition to faces new to the political scene, Clann also had many candidates from a republican background, including Kathleen Clarke, widow of Thomas Clarke, James Hilliard in Meath, Joseph McDevitt in Donegal West and Kevin Barry's brother Michael in Carlow-Kilkenny.

The three candidates in Limerick East typified the diverse elements of the electorate from which Clann was seeking to win support. Thomas Malone had taken part in the 1916 Rising and was, according to Clann literature, 'probably one of the youngest men interned in the United Kingdom'. He had served several terms of imprisonment in

Cork, Dundalk and Mountjoy, from where, along with nineteen comrades, he had 'made a sensational escape in the spring of 1919'. A second candidate in Limerick East, Seán O'Carroll, also came from a republican background. He had been associated with the Gaelic League since 1903 and had played with the Limerick All-Ireland teams of 1910–11. The third candidate, G. E. (Ted) Russell looked to a different category of voters, those who would support the party for its socio-economic agenda. Russell was born in 1911 and local newspapers reported that he had 'extensive business interests' in Limerick. At the time of the 1948 election he was president of the local Chamber of Commerce.

In a number of other constituencies Clann also attempted to include candidates who would embody the republican and welfarist elements it represented. In Sligo-Leitrim one candidate, accountancy student Patrick Kiernan from Carrigallen in County Leitrim, was the son of the manager of the local branch of the Ulster Bank. He was joined on the ticket by John Leonard, who had joined the Volunteers in 1918 and served time in Dartmoor. Indeed, like several other Clann candidates, Leonard had previous political associations. He had been elected to Sligo County Council for Fianna Fáil in 1942.

Many other candidates, like Noel Hartnett, had been members of the other parties prior to the formation of Clann. Seán McCool in Donegal East had contested the 1943 general election as an independent candidate, as had Margaret Anne Ashe in Galway West. Michael Hardy in Mayo North had been an unsuccessful Fianna Fáil candidate in 1943. Clann's candidate in Louth, Aodh de Blácam, had been co-opted on to the Fianna Fáil national executive in July 1946 at the time when Clann was formed. He was instrumental in having a sub-committee of the national executive established to examine the causes and consequences of rural depopulation. He also wrote articles in the *Irish Press* under the pen name 'Roddy the Rover'. De Blácam, who was to become press officer at the Department of Health when Noël Browne was Minister, resigned from Fianna Fáil on 1 December 1947. A month later his name was on the ballot paper for Clann na Poblachta in Louth. Whether the addition of such late converts was good for Clann is debatable, but the party was glad of such new members.

As the election campaign began, the deficiencies in the organisation of the party became evident. There was a degree of confusion over candidate selection. In Limerick East one man whose name had been mentioned as a prospective Clann candidate wrote to the *Limerick Leader* in mid-December to state: 'I am not a member of Clann na Poblachta and do not intend to become one.' The Cork edition of the *Kerryman* on 24 January reported that Clann 'staged a last minute surprise by the nomination of a second candidate for the North Cork constituency'. Ned Reilly had been selected for Clann in Tipperary South but in a letter to local newspapers in early January, it was stated that he had withdrawn for health reasons. This statement was soon countered by Reilly himself declaring that he 'certainly withdrew from Clann na Poblachta but not for health reasons'.

In Meath, the assistant county surveyor of the local

county council, who had been selected to run for the party, withdrew his name for 'personal reasons'. In the *Clare Champion* newspaper a letter appeared from a Thomas Gardiner, in which he stated that he was not acting as the party's director of canvassing in the constituency, as had been stated in an earlier edition. Gardiner said he had never accepted such a position and had not even been present at the Clann meeting at which, it was reported, he had been appointed.

This kind of confusion evident in the party organisation in several constituencies sums up much of what was wrong with Clann at the time. The reality was that Clann was poorly prepared to challenge the other political parties despite having candidates in every constituency. After the by-election victories Clann gained a profile and began to attract new members. In parts of the country where it had had no active organisation, local units were formed. For instance, a series of meetings held in Clare throughout November and December were reported to have been 'largely attended'. The *Clare Champion* reported on 13 December that Clann was said to be 'exceptionally active but, although several names have been mentioned, no step has yet been taken officially for the selection of a candidate'. By the time Clann's convention in Clare was scheduled to take place during Christmas week, the leaders of the other parties had addressed meetings in the constituency, accompanied by their candidates. Clann was slow getting started not only in Clare but in many other constituencies. This poor organisation was to continue into the New Year and up to polling day at the end of January.

The Clare convention, first organised for Christmas week of 1947, eventually took place on 4 January 1948. It was reported that the convention was attended by 150 delegates, representing thirty-eight affiliated branches. Local newspapers reported that 'after a lengthy discussion it was agreed that three candidates should be put forward'. However, an advertisement for Clann in the *Clare Champion* on 10 January listed four candidates, Peter O'Loughlin, Thomas Lillis, Tim Smythe and Noel Hartnett. It was noted in an article in the paper that: 'Mr Hartnett has also been selected for a Dublin constituency. It is stated that in the event of his being nominated in Clare, one of the others named will not go forward.' Hartnett eventually stood in the Dun Laoghaire-Rathdown constituency and the other three listed were the candidates in Clare.

Among the candidates were many founding members of the party who had served on the National Executive: Thomas Roycroft in Cork West, Fionán Breathnach in Dublin North-Central, Peadar Cowan in Dublin North-East, Michael Fitzpatrick in Dublin North-West, Con Lehane in Dublin South-Central, Donal O'Donoghue in Dublin South-East, Richard Batterberry, May Laverty in Dublin South-West, as well as Noel Hartnett. It was clear from the constituencies they contested that a large proportion of Clann's leading members were based in Dublin.

About half the candidates selected by Clann were from the professional classes. They included nineteen teachers, thirteen lawyers and ten doctors. The business community was represented by twenty-three candidates and there were also a number of farmers. Later on it became clear that many of the candidates selected were ill-suited to the constituencies in which they ran. Indeed, the *Limerick Leader* of 31 January accurately summed up what was to be Clann's eventual dilemma: 'Unfortunately for his party, it has not been organised sufficiently long to enable it to select or attract many candidates who have either Mr MacBride's popular personality or background.' Cork was a notably weak spot, where Clann encountered particular resistance especially from local republicans. Indeed, the subsequent election results proved just how badly organised Clann was in Cork city and county.

All this was still weeks away as party members embarked on a journey which they believed would led to the replacement of the Fianna Fáil government of Éamon de Valera by a Clann na Poblachta government headed up by Taoiseach Seán MacBride. Throughout November and December Clann continued the process of organising in the constituencies. A meeting in Lucan on 22 November was reported to be 'largely attended', while a gathering in Kildare the following day resulted in some fifty people joining the party. They heard Kevin Costello, a party activist from Dublin, declare that 'Clann na Poblachta was not interested in fighting the civil war all over again . . . '

Patrick Brennan, a farmer and rate collector who was the party's candidate in Kildare, appealed to young people. Those, he said, who 'were not born twenty-five years ago but who are shut out of public life because you did not take part in the disastrous civil war of 1922 are welcome into the ranks of the Clann'. This was a theme which Clann candidates and speakers took up at meetings throughout the country over the following weeks. The party's General Secretary, Michael A. Kelly, told an election meeting in Castlerea that the 'old cry of 'where were you in 1916 and 1921?' was gone and the cry the next day would be: 'where will you be tomorrow?' Kelly, who himself had strong republican links, was the party candidate in Roscommon.

Clann candidates were nonetheless not averse to evoking the republican names from years gone by. The *Leinster Leader* reported Patrick Brennan as claiming that Clann 'policy is formulated with the ideas of all the great national leaders of the past - of Tone, Emmet, Fintan Lawlor, of the 1916 patriots'. The party's candidate in Donegal West, Joseph McDevitt, had according to his election literature been 'five times wounded in the fight for independence, was twice sentenced to death and was in the precincts of seventeen jails. He did ten months solitary confinement and took part in three hunger strikes.' With republican links and local associations so important in Irish politics at the time, McDevitt, who was also chairman of the county GAA board, must have been a strong candidate.

It is generally accepted that Clann had a sizeable debt after the 1948 general election. Money was raised for the campaign from business people and voluntary membership subscriptions. In addition, Clann's two existing TDs had to give an allowance to the party. The party's treasurer wrote to most newspapers in the first week of 1948 to 'acknowledge receipt of the following sums of money from Mr S. MacBride, TD., £109 0s 8d., Patrick Kinnane, TD., £109 0s 8d., which represents the amounts received by them as salary since their election to Dáil Éireann'. She used the letter to promote Clann policy, stating that both deputies had 'voluntarily handed over their salaries to Clann na Poblachta expressing their desire that they did not wish to make any personal gain out of the discharge of their duties'.

The chairman of the Clare constituency selection convention, held in the Queen's Hotel in Ennis, told delegates that he had been instructed by the standing committee to the effect that each candidate should pledge him/herself that, if and when elected, s/he would hand to the treasurer of Clann na Poblachta his/her entire salary as a Dáil deputy. S/he would then be reimbursed for all expenses and loss of business by the party's central fund. Seán MacBride told a meeting in Limerick in early January that he 'had a strong objection to the creation of a class of professional politician dependent on the public for a livelihood'.

It can only be surmised that some of the money raised was used to fund party election activities throughout the country. Clann produced its own propaganda, with the first issue of a four-page bulletin appearing in early December. It was circulated with a cover price of one penny and was entitled *The Clann*. Nine issues were produced on a weekly basis until the beginning of February.

In addition to the bulletin, a film about Clann was made featuring Browne, Hartnett and MacBride. They travelled to London, where the film was produced in Ealing Studios.

It sought to outline the objectives of the party. According to Browne 'the film showed the suffering and poverty in which the mass of our people, especially in city tenements, were living; high unemployment, forced emigration, widespread uncontrolled tuberculosis'. It was generally shown on gable walls prior to speeches. A record of speeches made by MacBride, Hartnett and Browne was also put on sale. On this record Noel Hartnett appealed to the electorate for support to build a new Ireland: 'I ask you not to listen to the petty objections and differences raised by the men of small minds. I ask you to believe that moral fervour and honest effort can overcome all difficulties . . . '

In his recorded speech, Seán MacBride claimed that Clann was the first real attempt since the Civil War to raise national affairs out of the rut of party politics and bitterness. He returned to his familiar refrain that politics over the previous quarter of a century had been dominated by personalities and by individuals associated with the Independence movement. This was MacBride's shorthand for an attack on Éamon de Valera. As was the case in previous campaigns, an examination of speeches delivered at rallies in constituencies throughout the country indicates that the Clann leader never laid any blame for the country's economic and political ills directly at the door of Éamon de Valera.

The nearest MacBride came to attacking de Valera was at a party meeting in Kilrush in County Clare. The Clann leader was on what was described in local newspapers as 'a swift tour of County Clare'. He told the Kilrush meeting that de Valera deserved well of the people but that over the previous ten to fifteen years the electorate had voted for the man rather than the party. He said it was 'sad that such a man, who did so much for the country, should stoop to methods in this election that are unworthy of any responsible leader'. On another occasion, MacBride argued that the 'country had suffered from having too much personal leadership'. It seems likely that Clann had taken a policy decision not to attack the Fianna Fáil leader personally lest this should cause a backlash against the new party. It concentrated instead on winning the support of the electorate away from the Fianna Fáil party. For instance, the party's candidate in Roscommon, Jack McQuillan, a county footballer and building contractor, told his electorate that under Fianna Fáil, 'political life was based on past events and personalities rather than on policies'.

In the recording Seán MacBride again appealed to young people to support Clann. 'The young people . . . the people who with no national record came to feel that public affairs did not concern them, that politics was a monopoly of a small clique'. The Clann leader spoke of the need for a vision and a policy for the future. He argued that 'the present government has been fifteen years in office, they have lost their idealism, they have become lazy and dictatorial. I have no wish to say bitter things about them, many of them deserve well of the people but the time definitely has come when a new outlook . . . is necessary.' MacBride described Clann as a party which had 'a policy that provides a new deal for a new generation. It places before you men of ability, honesty and integrity - give them your support'.

Noël Browne took as the theme of his broadcast the need to improve medical treatment and facilities. 'Only two out of the existing so-called forty-two sanatoria provide full treatment facilities. The result is that nearly four and a half thousand people die every year of TB. Nine hundred and fifty are waiting in vain for admission to these sanatoria. TB is now preventable and curable. Why then have nearly sixty thousand people died of this disease in the last fifteen years?'

As well as making use of the film and the long-playing record, it was reported that members of Clann 'toured the towns with a loudspeaker-carrying van and broadcast recorded speeches of leading party personalities.' The *Leinster Leader* noted that 'the platform was equipped with a most elaborate public address loudspeaking apparatus'. These loudspeakers were not always put to the best use. One local paper reported that Fianna Fáil's 'Erskine Childers had such a fantastic harangue with Noel Hartnett through the medium of loudspeaker vans that their respective meetings became a farce'.

The *Offaly Independent* proclaimed that 'electioneering history' had been made when a Clann-sponsored aeroplane, a three-seater Proctor, went from one end of the country to the other. Whether or not this was history is not clear, as Fianna Fáil also had an aeroplane to spread its message. The value of all these election gimmicks was questioned in the *Sligo Champion* which wrote: 'The Fianna Fáil propaganda aeroplane which flew over Sligo during the day attracted scant attention and many people were unaware of its election association until they read a morning paper next day'. An advertisement in the same newspaper said of Clann's election programme - 'Some of Ireland's best brains have helped to make this plan. For your sake and your children's, hear it, study it - VOTE FOR IT.' Throughout the campaign Clann traded under the banner of 'Put them out' as the election became very much the rest versus Fianna Fáil, with Fianna Fáil versus Clann na Poblachta.

Clann's 1948 general election campaign also inspired poetry. The *Tipperary Star* published a lyric from an 'agricultural worker's wife' from Clonmel. It was entitled 'Under One Flag?'

> Good-bye de Valera, - and Seán Mac Entee,
> Who gave us the brown bread and half ounce of tea,
> We are saying 'good-bye to them all',
> As out of the Dáil they must crawl.
> We'll give them 'the pension',
> When they stand to 'attention',
> So vote Clann na Poblachta, all.
>
> Come on MacBride, the brave and true,
> Few men in the Dáil could equal you,
> For me, I know you'll do your best
> God speed you to victory with the rest.

As a result of the by-elections, Fianna Fáil was fully aware of the potential of the new party to take seats throughout the country. The government party was not prepared to sit back as Clann went out seeking votes but went on the offensive. It had foreseen the possibility of Clann's appeal to middle-class voters. A series of weekly advertisements was placed in *The Irish Times* aimed at attracting this sector of the electorate. This 'information series', as it was called, dealt with issues such as prices, price control and the value of tourism.

Fianna Fáil also used its position in government to introduce measures in an attempt to make life a little easier for the public. A new housing bill was introduced in mid-November, which provided grants for people who wished to build their own houses. As Fianna Fáil launched its campaign, Seán Lemass introduced an order reducing the price of meat. In mid-December the butter ration was increased from four to six ounces with effect from early January. Controls on coal and firewood were also removed. At election rallies throughout the country Fianna Fáil speakers described an economy which was turning the corner to better, more prosperous times. Éamon de Valera told one rally in Cork he believed 'a large number of those who went away will come back'. He also claimed that much emigration was 'only temporary'.

Throughout the election campaign Clann bore the brunt of Fianna Fáil attacks. With the likelihood that Clann would not secure an overall majority but would have to share power, the government party also turned its attention to the alleged vices of coalition administrations. Fianna Fáil repeatedly questioned the stability of a coalition government and in its advertisements asked 'Who would be Taoiseach?' In January, at a rally in Limerick city, Éamon de Valera proclaimed: 'You do not know whether it will be fish, flesh or good red herring. You don't know who the members of the government will be, and that won't come until the election is over'.

The 'red scare' tactic was used to the full by Fianna Fáil to create doubt in people's minds about Clann's origins and future intentions. At a meeting in Kilkenny in early January Seán Lemass told his audience that 'international communism might come to Ireland under the guise of nationalism'. Clann was worried that if it responded to Fianna Fáil's insinuations of a communist threat it would distract the electorate from the main issues. In reality it had no choice but to respond to Fianna Fáil's accusations and every speech made by MacBride contained dismissals of alleged communist influences. At the party's final electoral rally in Limerick, it was reported that he 'received a tremendous reception'. MacBride argued that Clann's 'policy is based on the social and economic encyclicals and I challenge anybody to find anything in our programme which conflicts in any way with Catholic social and economic thinking'. He went on to tell what the *Limerick Leader* described as a 'huge public meeting' that 'Clann na Poblachta believed and laid down the right of the Irish people to live, to marry and to bring up families in reasonable Christian comfort in their own country . . . '

Despite the words of the party leader, Clann candidates throughout the country were obviously worried that the smear campaign was proving effective for Fianna Fáil. One of the party's speakers at a rally in Monaghan took exception to Fianna Fáil's claim that Clann was communist. He declared himself 'a Catholic, of Catholic parents and would have nothing to do with a Communist Party'. The *Democrat and People's Journal* noted that Clann speakers received 'a receptive audience at all meetings except Lower Magheracloone where the people hurried home after an early Mass'. Whether or not their hurry was caused by something they heard in church is not stated.

One of Clann's candidates in the Louth constituency, Aodh de Blácam, took up the same topic at a rally in Dundalk in a downpour. He declared that Clann 'stood on the principles of papal encyclicals and the social plan of the Bishop of Clonfert, so if they were communists, so was the pope himself'. However, references to bishops and popes could not take from the fact that Clann could not count on any neutral endorsement from the religious. While there was no direct attack by the Catholic Church on the country's newest political party, oblique references conveyed the Church's point of view. One example was when the Bishop of Cashel, addressing the employees of the Sugar Beet Factory in Thurles, warned of the dangers of communist agents known to be operating in Ireland. The message was clear for all those who wanted to hear.

The electoral contest in the Meath constituency was interesting as one of Clann's candidates was the brother of a sitting Fianna Fáil TD. Prior to joining Clann James Hilliard, a dairy farmer, had been an independent republican member of Meath County Council. His brother Michael was also a veteran of the independence struggle. He had first been elected to the Dáil in 1943 and later went on to serve in a number of Fianna Fáil cabinets. Despite his brother's affiliations with Clann, Michael Hilliard described the policy of that party as 'fantastic and incapable of being carried out to its logical conclusion'. The danger of the communist slur influencing voters was also of concern to James Hilliard. The *Meath Chronicle* reported the Clann candidate telling a meeting in Kells that 'a Dublin priest had told him that among the executive of Clann na Poblachta were some of the best Catholics in Dublin'.

In order to appeal to a broad constituency it was necessary for Clann to extend its range of policies. In many ways Clann was adopting the position of a catch-all party in the mould of Fainna Fáil but the failure of the party to identify its core objective at an earlier date left it open to abuse from opponents, such as Fianna Fáil's red scare campaign.

The party suffered some embarrassing internal confusion about the issues it actually represented. In early December, Peadar Cowan stated that Clann in power would rescind the sentences handed down to republican prisoners and re-structure the legal system. Although Clann members would have been supportive of such policies neither suggestion was actually part of the party's publicly declared programme. As Cowan was a senior party member the ambiguity left the way open for Fianna Fáil to attack Clann. Fianna Fáil speakers were able to suggest that there were serious internal divisions over policy among some of Clann's most senior members. Cowan was a popular member of the party's National Executive and a candidate in Dublin North-East. He saw himself as a minister in any future Clann government. Clann members and candidates defended his name against Fianna Fáil attacks, especially accusations that he was a communist. James Hilliard in Meath supported his colleague, saying that Cowan 'was the father of eleven children and a very good practising Catholic'.

Given the republican background of many Clann supporters and candidates another potential Achilles heel for the party was the North. Throughout the general election campaign Seán MacBride stuck firmly to previously enunciated policy on the North. The Clann leader spoke of the need to open up the Oireachtas to elected representatives of the Six Counties. He reiterated Clann policy that until such time as social and economic standards in the Twenty-Six Counties were at least on a par with those in the North, 'it would be impossible to invite the Nationalist elements to throw their lot in with ours'.

Like the other party leaders, Seán MacBride went on tour, addressing electoral rallies in constituencies. From the coverage in the various local newspapers it is obvious that the Clann leader was well received and provided the new party with a major credibility bonus. In his speeches MacBride concentrated to a large extent on the general economic situation. A torchlight procession with three bands led him into Dundalk in early January. It was reported that he was received by a crowd which was 'attentive but not demonstrative'. He told them: 'The War of Independence was not fought for the purpose of changing the colour of their flag or changing the occupants of Government Buildings. It was fought to establish the freedom of the people and their rights to bring up their children in reasonable comfort.'

In an RTÉ interview with John Bowman in the 1970s, MacBride said, 'My director of elections complained that I spoke too much about economics but I felt it was necessary that I explain the essentials of the economic problems which faced the country.' It may be that this concentration on Clann's economic proposals did not help candidates to convey their message clearly. One pre-election editorial in the *Limerick Leader* noted that Clann's monetary policy 'could not but produce chaos and disaster . . . ' Throughout the country Clann candidates made speeches concentrating on the Government's economic performance. One of the party's three candidates in Clare, Tim Smythe, declared 'the slogan of Cromwell was "to hell or to Connaught" and nowadays the slogan of Fianna Fáil for the young people could very well be "To hell or to England".'

Coming up to polling day Clann supporters were optimistic. MacBride is reported in the *Limerick Weekly Echo* as stating he 'would not be surprised if there was a veritable landslide' for his party. Those associated with Clann were confidently predicting the party would win between forty-five and seventy-five seats. But the election results did not herald a Clann breakthrough. There was to be no landslide. While for a new party in its general election début the results were creditable, for those closely associated with Clann the outcome proved a bitter disappointment. One member said she would 'never forget listening to results coming in on the radio and in places Clann, instead of being at the head of the poll, were at the bottom . . . it was just unbelievable . . . '

Prominent names failed all over the country: Patrick McCartan in Cork, Aodh de Blacám, alias Roddy the Rover, in Louth, and May Laverty in Dublin. Donal O'Donoghue, the chairman of the party's National Executive, received only 500 votes in Dublin South-East although at least Clann had the consolation of seeing Noël Browne elected in that constituency.

The party did well in the Dublin constituencies. Noël Browne's three-seat constituency also returned John A. Costello and Seán MacEntee. MacBride topped the poll in Dublin South-West. In Dun Laoghaire-Rathdown, with just over 3,800 first-preference votes, Joseph Brennan polled almost six hundred votes more than his party colleague Noel Hartnett. This was enough for Brennan to stay ahead of Hartnett and take one of the three seats on offer in that constituency.

In Dublin North-East Peadar Cowan put behind him several previous unsuccessful attempts to win a Dáil seat for the Labour Party. He was joined in the Dáil by Michael Fitzpatrick in Dublin North-West and by Con Lehane. As well as the six TDs elected in Dublin constituencies, Clann had successes in Cavan, Roscommon, Tipperary South and Tipperary North. John Tully in Cavan was to prove the most durable of Clann's elected representatives, surviving at all general elections but one until the party was eventually dissolved in the mid-1960s. Patrick Kinnane was re-elected, topping the poll in the new Tipperary North constituency. The fact that the by-election had been contested for the whole of Tipperary the previous October obviously helped

John Timoney. He was one of three Clann candidates in the new Tipperary South constituency and took the last seat in this four-seater. The recent constituency changes had also increased the Roscommon constituency to a four-seater. Jack McQuillan took that extra seat for Clann and became the youngest member elected to the Dáil in the 1948 general election.

Clann won ten Dáil seats and no party had an overall majority. Fine Gael saw its share of the vote fall below 20 per cent for the first time, but the party still managed to pick up one extra seat. With sixty-eight deputies, Fianna Fáil found itself six seats short of the elusive Dáil majority. The two Labour groupings had between them nineteen seats, while seven Clann na Talmhan candidates had been returned. The independents, from an array of backgrounds, won twelve seats. Initially it was expected that Fianna Fáil would form a minority government with the external support of a number of Independents and possibly of the National Labour grouping.

One interesting aside from the results was reported in the *Clare Champion*. It was said there were fewer comments written on the ballot papers than in previous elections. The views of one voter, however, summed up the issues concerning most people. The message on the ballot paper went ' . . . hope that whoever is elected will give us twice as much flour as we are getting now'.

Regardless of voters' comments, in the end Fianna Fáil's electoral revision had achieved the desired result. Clann would have won nineteen seats rather than ten, had it secured representation proportional to its vote. Clann won 13.3 per cent of the first-preference votes but only 6.8 per cent of the contested seats. Fifteen constituencies proved to be marginal ones for the party. In three of those constituencies Clann won seats, and with a little more luck another five seats could have come Clann's way.

For such a new party the support won in many constituencies was very good but it was just short of that required to win extra seats. In twenty-four out of the forty constituencies, the Clann vote ranged between 0.5 and 0.9 quotas. Despite this the party took seats in only six of these constituencies. One of the factors influencing this was that Clann's candidates did not attract cross-party preferences, perhaps because many of Clann's candidates were new to the electorate. However, Clann also took some seats which its share of the vote should not have allowed it to win. The *Tipperary Star* said John Timoney should have been 'regarded as lucky to get so far'. With the assistance of Clann na Talmhan transfers Timoney took a Fianna Fáil seat by five hundred votes.

One of the most remarkable features of the Irish electoral system is the high retention rate of transfers by Fianna Fáil. On average over 80 per cent of electoral votes transferred from Fianna Fáil candidates have gone to other Fianna Fáil candidates who are available to receive transfers. TCD political scientist Michael Gallagher noted in an article in the *Economic and Social Review* that such high solidarity is a sign that a party is well organised. A lower solidarity indicates a weaker organisation, where candidates rely on votes on their own merits as much as on the party's appeal. The level of solidarity for smaller parties would generally be expected to be lower. In fact, Clann's rate in 1948 was fairly high for such a new party; nearly 70 per cent of its transfers remained within the party fold. But because Clann was a new party, supporters of other parties did not tend to give Clann candidates lower preference votes. This was one of the real reasons for the party's disproportionately low share of Dáil seats.

This shortcoming in Clann's performance was because the party had not moved quickly enough since its formation in July 1946 to put in place throughout the country a genuine organisational structure. In many constituencies the party was not even organised when Éamon de Valera indicated his intention to seek an early general election. In attempting to shake Fianna Fáil's tight hold on power by contesting every constituency Clann overstretched its organis-ation and dissipated support. The strategy of running so many candidates also proved costly. The election results showed this without doubt when forty-eight of the party's ninety-three candidates lost their deposits.

Clann also paid inadequate attention to candidate selection. The party's leaders had been slow in identifying suitable candidates. Most of its candidates were politically inexperienced. Where Clann did make a break-through it was because a candidate benefited from a personal vote or received the backing of a large disgruntled element of the local electorate. MacBride, Cowan and Lehane were three well-known names who succeeded. Other successful candidates like Kinnane in Tipperary, Tully in Cavan and McQuillan in Roscommon were individuals with strong local links which tapped into a republican background or an association with Gaelic games.

There were many examples of candidates who were simply the wrong choice. One of the party's candidates in Carlow-Kilkenny was Charles Sheehan. Although he was a native of Piltown he was teaching in Dublin and living in Drumcondra. He published an apology in the *Kilkenny People* in the week before polling day saying that he would 'not be able to address meetings arranged for Saturday and Sunday as he has been engaged to speak at meetings in other constituencies'. Clann had two other candidates in Carlow-Kilkenny. One was Carlow-based Michael Barry, a brother of the executed hero Kevin Barry. He had previously stood for election as an Anti-Treaty Candidate in 1926. The third candidate, Patrick Gleeson from Kilkenny, was a 'druggist by profession' and had been interned in 1936 and 1940. He was to remain a party activist over the following years and served as Mayor of Kilkenny. When the general election results were known the local newspaper, the *Kilkenny People*, noted: 'there was, of course, some surprise that Clann na Poblachta failed to secure a seat . . . ' However, the fact that one of its three candidates was not living in the constituency and spent crucial days canvassing in other constituencies could not have helped the party's cause.

The failure of Clann to fulfil expectations had been forecast in some newspapers. The *Nationalist and Leinster Times*, in the first week of January, said that Clann 'is not the threat of a well organised or established political party, as the one which defeated Mr Cosgrave's in 1932'. A month later, after the election results were known, the newspaper's editorial returned to the same topic. Drawing comparisons with Fianna Fáil's performance in 1932 the paper wrote: 'One has little doubt that the process would have been repeated had there been a better organised Clann na Poblachta with a spectacular policy and candidates who endorsed it at every street corner'. The newspaper observed that 'many who went to the polls asked themselves what fundamental differences there were between Fianna Fáil and Clann na Poblachta'. The results would appear to indicate that many voters could not identify any great difference.

Nevertheless, a number of other local newspapers expressed surprise that Clann's overall election performance had not been better. The *Sligo Champion* noted: 'One of the biggest surprises of the count was the low poll received by the Clann na Poblachta candidates whose joint total number of first preferences was 4,287, a little more than half the quota.' One of the candidates, Plunkett Flanagan, in a speech delivered when the outcome was known, said: 'The results were disappointing as far as Clann na Poblachta were concerned and were very hard to explain in view of the enthusiasm shown all over the country. The general view seemed to be that the party and the men who were in it were too young but it was hoped to fight another day.' Flanagan, who was a merchant in Sligo, also said: 'The general view seemed to be one of distrust of the more voluntary aspects of our programme. We will now be in a position to form a very virile opposition'.

Prior to polling day the *Leinster Leader* had reported on a 'largely attended and enthusiastic meeting' in the Kildare constituency. After the votes were counted and it was evident that Clann's candidates had performed poorly, the same newspaper observed the 'most remarkable of all was the poor vote cast for the Clann na Poblachta representatives, who were frankly disappointed at the returns.' Although Jack McQuillan took a seat in Roscommon the local newspaper, the *Roscommon Champion*, noted that the 'outstanding feature of the election was the complete collapse of Clann na Poblachta as a serious party contestant'.

Everywhere, commentators and Clann supporters looked for reasons for the party's failure to make its mark in as dramatic a manner as Fianna Fáil in 1932. The communist threat must certainly have played a part. The publication of the Locke Tribunal Report in mid-December 1947 was good news for Fianna Fáil. The report found that the corruption changes against the government were without foundation. This conclusion served to restore Fianna Fáil's image and made many of Clann's accusations about corruption in high places less credible.

The loss of so many young people through emigration obviously fed through to the electorate, which as a consequence had acquired an older profile. Maurice Manning, in his book on Irish political parties, wrote of 'the innate conservatism of the Irish electorate'. The impact of large-scale emigration on Clann's vote can only be estimated. If an older profile is associated with a more conservative viewpoint, the responsiveness of the electorate to Clann's new message must have been reduced. Addressing the negative socio-economic forces behind emigration was part of Clann's agenda but the people most affected by those forces were in London and other British and American cities. They were not available throughout the country to cast their votes for Clann.

The accusations levelled against the party by Fianna Fáil hurt many candidates. One of the Kildare candidates was Dr Daniel Boland, the assistant Master of Holles Street Hospital in Dublin, and a sportsman who had made the trial for the international rugby team. In a speech after the final results were declared in his constituency, Boland said he 'bitterly resented the accusation of Communism' made against Clann. Jack McQuillan alluded to the newness of the party but told his supporters that Clann was 'there to stay' and intended immediately to organise in 'every nook and corner not only in Roscommon but in the whole of Ireland.'

Clann's 1948 support has been described as 'twin-peaked' because the party won votes from traditional anti-partitionist republicans in rural areas and from urban radicals. Only four of Clann's ten seats were won outside Dublin and two of these were in Tipperary. In comparison with stances adopted by other republican movements over the previous twenty-five years, Clann's policy on the North was not that radical. It could be that this proved a problem in some rural constituencies, especially along the western seaboard and the border with Northern Ireland. It was in these areas that Clann failed to make any serious inroads into the Fianna Fáil vote. The very fact that constituencies like Longford-

Westmeath and Monaghan were prepared to return Sinn Féin candidates espousing an abstentionist policy at the 1957 general election must raise the question of the electorate's acceptance of Clann's republican agenda a decade earlier.

Nevertheless, Clann's republican outlook suggested that most of its lower preferences would go to Fianna Fáil, while its vague radicalism and sense of grievance at social issues would suggest a high transfer to Labour. Since Fine Gael seemed both conservative and pro-Commonwealth, a very low transfer to that party would have been expected. However, as the table on page 88 shows, these expectations were not fulfilled.

When both Fianna Fáil and Fine Gael candidates were available to receive transfers from Clann candidates, almost twice as many Clann votes went to Fine Gael as to Fianna Fáil. This figure is surprising, although it must be qualified by the observation that about two-thirds of the transfers went to neither of these parties. When the analysis is confined to situations where candidates from the three main parties were available to receive Clann transfers, a clear preference for Labour emerged. One possible explanation of these patterns is that, whatever the reservations of Clann supporters about Fine Gael and Labour, the strength of hostility felt towards the Fianna Fáil government transcended all other factors.

Transfers from Clann na Poblachta, 1948 General Election			
Election	Transfer from	Parties always available to receive transfers	Percentage of transfers received from each group
1948	Clann	Fianna Fáil Fine Gael	Fianna Fáil 11.9 Fine Gael 23.2 Others 32.9 Non-Transferable 32.0
1948	Clann	Fianna Fáil Fine Gael Labour	Fianna Fáil 10.0 Fine Gael 18.1 Labour 39.5 Others 10.3 Non-Transferable 22.2

Source: Gallagher, 1978

Fianna Fáil voters tend to 'plump' on their ballot papers: that is, they list no other preferences after voting for all the Fianna Fáil candidates. It is generally accepted that 'plumping' is one way for voters to convey their contempt for all candidates of non-favoured parties. Nearly 40 per cent of Clann votes became non-transferable in situations where no other Clann candidates were available to receive those transfers. The evidence would suggest that Clann won over discontented supporters from all parties but much of its support of this kind was an electoral protest against the established political parties. This situation would be to the disadvantage of Clann later on.

There was understandable disappointment with the general election result within Clann circles. In a later RTÉ radio interview, Seán MacBride declared:

> Up to a fortnight before polling we certainty
> would have got 40 seats . . . in the last fortnight
> I could feel the tide slipping away from us -
> this was partly due to a number of scare stories
> that we would nationalise the banks, that the
> people's savings wouldn't be safe, that we were
> communists or near-communists, every kind
> of rumour was set going about Clann, princip-
> ally by the Fianna Fáil party, and also to a
> certain extent by the *Irish Times* . . .

For a new party Clann had no need to be despondent about its performance. One journalist, Barney Boland, writing in the *Nationalist and Leinster Times,* said it would have been easy to overrate Clann's failure. He pinpointed the reason for the party's less than spectacular performance. Boland considered Clann too 'ill-prepared and ill-disciplined, lacking clear aims or a consistent policy'.

Interestingly, Barney Boland found fault with the role adopted by Seán MacBride throughout the election campaign. 'For hundreds of years the Irish people have been determinedly making their leaders into heroes, whether they deserve it or not.' Boland believed MacBride needed to come to terms with this reality 'or else abandon his aspiration to political leadership in the state'.

Brian Inglis of *The Irish Times* wrote that Seán MacBride 'was not impressive on the platform. His face, skull-like in its contours, split rather than relaxed by his rare smile, was a little intimidating: and the foreign inflection was not attractive on the hustings as it could be in conversation.' Inglis also wrote that MacBride spoke 'without relish or subtlety of . . . the repatriation of Ireland's assets and afforestation'. The reality was that Seán MacBride, for all his undoubted skills, was like most Clann members new to the political process. He lacked, as became evident in the inter-party government, the experience to lead the new political party, Clann na Poblachta.

In the end, the 1948 general election results left Fianna Fáil six seats short of an overall majority. Clann was faced with three options: remaining on the opposition benches, entering government with Fianna Fáil or joining some multi-party formation which would include Fine Gael and Labour.

4

BREAKING THE MOULD:
INTO GOVERNMENT

The general election had been held on Wednesday 4 February 1948, but delays meant the results became clear only some six days later. The constituency review process had increased the number of Dáil seats by nine – over the previous general election in 1944 – to one hundred and forty-seven. The election outcome left Fianna Fáil with sixty-eight seats, Fine Gael took thirty-one seats, with the combined Labour parties returning nineteen deputies. Clann na Talmhan had seven seats, and there were twelve independents and ten Clann deputies. The National Labour grouping was under strong internal and external pressure to support a minority Fianna Fáil government. It had five seats, sufficient to put Éamon de Valera back in the Taoiseach's office. Indeed, for a time it was believed Fianna Fáil would return to power in a minority administration supported by some Labour deputies and a number of the independents. However, as those in the other parties examined the election outcome it became obvious that alternative combinations were possible.

Clann members were still disappointed with their electoral

performance. Nevertheless, achieving power was still a possibility whether through entering government with Fianna Fáil or joining some multi-party formation involving Fine Gael and Labour. The Fianna Fáil route was never really considered. Initially Seán MacBride floated the idea of a national government comprised of members of all the different groupings in Dáil Éireann. Later he said:

> We had been elected on the basis of bringing about a change in government. Our most effective poster during the campaign was a three-word poster - 'Put them out'. It was on that basis that we had secured election. Once you were elected you have to bear the responsibility of taking decisions. The first decision we had to take was who do we vote for as Taoiseach. Obviously we ourselves couldn't hope to secure a majority. Therefore, the choice was limited to either Fine Gael or Fianna Fáil or the formation of an inter-party government. We couldn't logically vote for Fianna Fáil, it had given no indication of a willingness to moderate its then existing policies. We certainly didn't feel like voting for a Fine Gael government with whom we were not in tune ... therefore my first suggestion was the formation of a national government, Fianna Fáil and Fine Gael and Labour and ourselves ... This was turned down and the next alternative was the formation of a inter-party government ...

Fine Gael took the initiative in discussions on the formation of a government. The prime mover within Fine Gael was party leader Richard Mulcahy who was determined to force Fianna Fáil out of government. It was apparent that the only way to end Fianna Fáil's sixteen years in power was for the disparate groups to come together. The day after the final results were known, Mulcahy wrote to the leaders of the other four parties inviting them to a meeting to discuss options. This meeting took place in Leinster House on Friday 13 February.

The idea of some form of coalition government was not new. It had been discussed prior to the election in the Labour Party's official newspaper. At that time, however, the proposal was for a tri-party government between Labour, Clann na Talmhan and Clann na Poblachta. There was no mention of Fine Gael but the numbers game after the election meant Fine Gael had to be considered if any alternative government to Fianna Fáil was to be formed.

All the parties attended the meeting in Leinster House with the exception of National Labour, which was still considering approaches from Fianna Fáil to support it as a minority administration. From the outset it was clear that because of his background Richard Mulcahy was unacceptable as Taoiseach to elements in the proposed government. Mulcahy had been the IRA's Chief-of-Staff during the War of Independence. After the killing of Michael Collins he assumed the position of Commander-in-Chief of the pro-Treaty forces. He was one of the most vocal members of the Cumann na nGaedheal government advocating the use of force against anti-Treaty republicans in the 1920s. This fact alone aroused hostility from many potential members of the inter-party government towards the Waterford-born leader of Fine Gael. In addition, Mulcahy's involvement in the Blueshirt Movement in the 1930s made it nearly impossible for Clann to continue discussions on the formation of any new government if he were the choice as Taoiseach.

This potential conflict over the selection of Taoiseach from within the ranks of the possible partners was quickly removed from the discussions. The Labour leader, William Norton, made it clear that his party would not accept the leader of any of the parties involved as Taoiseach. Professor Brian Farrell has suggested that 'this was almost certainly a tactful way of registering objection to Mulcahy's obvious claim to be Taoiseach'. Fine Gael supporters would have expected their man to be Taoiseach but Mulcahy gave an immediate assurance that he would not stand in the way of a genuine effort to form a government. It was also William Norton who suggested that Fine Gael Deputy for Dublin South-East, John A. Costello, attend future meetings to 'advise and help' their efforts in forming a government. Costello was a well-known and successful senior counsel. He had been Assistant Attorney General from 1923 until he was appointed to the top job of Attorney General in 1926, serving until Cumann na nGaedheal left office in 1932. Costello's involvement was accepted by all participants in the talks.

The parties met again the following day, 14 February. On this occasion the meeting was arranged for the Mansion

House. Among those present at this meeting were Mulcahy, Costello, Dillon and the other prospective ministers from Fine Gael, Labour, Clann na Talmhan and Clann na Poblachta. The structure and personnel of party representation in the cabinet were agreed in advance of addressing the question of who should be Taoiseach. It is believed that Seán MacBride suggested Fine Gael's John Esmonde of Wexford as Taoiseach but in the end John A. Costello was formally invited to become Taoiseach. The previous evening Costello had told colleagues he would not join the cabinet in an inter-party government and that he would agree 'in no circumstance' to become Attorney General. However, he went away from the Mansion House meeting with an invitation to succeed Éamon de Valera as Taoiseach. Having discussed the implications with family and friends, Costello agreed the following day to become Taoiseach. Clann members were not unhappy with his selection as Taoiseach. Seán MacBride knew the Fine Gael deputy from legal circles. Indeed, it is believed that Costello was one of those who had over a number of years persuaded MacBride to exchange his fringe republicanism for constitutional activity.

Clann members met for six hours the following day to decide on what course of action to take. The decision to enter a coalition government was not to the liking of everyone within the party. During the election campaign Dr Patrick McCartan said that 'so far as coalition government is concerned the question did not arise'. In addition, the inclusion of Fine Gael in the proposed government made many uneasy. Con Lehane had previously described Fine

Gael 'as a party with a murky past and no political future'. However, MacBride reasoned that as Clann's election slogan was 'Put Them Out' this was exactly what would be done to Fianna Fáil through the formation of the inter-party government.

It is understood that the vote of the Clann National Executive on whether or not to enter government was a close one. MacBride is believed to be the only one of the original thirteen IRA men from the executive to vote for entering government. Some prominent members later resigned from the party in protest, viewing a government involving Fine Gael as a betrayal. Noël Browne maintains that the party decided its best position was to choose the inter-party option, then help to make it work and eventually bring it down at an appropriate time for Clann to improve its electoral position.

Clann made a number of demands of the government it was about to enter. These appeared in *The Irish Times* of 16 February. They included the establishment of a council on emigration; adequate facilities to combat TB; a solution to the housing problem; an adequate social security plan; the removal of taxes on beer, tobacco and cinema seats; a reduction in the cost of living; a council on education; public control of state corporations; zoned agriculture and decentralisation of government. A number of prominent Clann policies were omitted from the shopping list, notably the repatriation of sterling assets and re-afforestation. Nor was there any specific reference to policy on Northern Ireland. Seán MacBride later defended Clann's approach to joining the government. 'As a minority party in the coalition I didn't feel that we had the right to make these major demands and anyway I felt that the logic of the situation would propel us towards the implementation of those policies without making a political issue of them'.

This new inter-party government was voted into power by the Dáil on 18 February, 1948. The *Leinster Leader* noted that when the first deputies came into the Dáil Chamber 'the public galleries were filled and behind the railings surrounding the members' seats, senators, former deputies and officials competed for seats'. The distinguished visitors' gallery was also packed with members of the diplomatic corps, led by Lord Rugby, the United Kingdom's representative in Ireland. When Seán MacBride led his deputies into the chamber they went towards the benches usually occupied by Independents and Labour members. However, they found that most of the seats were already occupied. Indeed, some Clann deputies ended up seated beside Fine Gael TDs, once the enemy but now their partners in government.

The Clann leader spoke on the nomination of John A. Costello as Taoiseach. He said the people had 'by 750,000 to 500,000 votes clearly indicated that they wished to terminate the virtual political monopoly which has existed for some sixteen years'. In his speech, MacBride also sought to allay the fears of Clann supporters who were less than enthusiastic about the new arrangement. He claimed the party would 'not abandon, waive, mitigate or abate . . . ' any part of its policy, but would 'merely agree to co-operate with the other parties . . . ' in the new government.

As head of the outgoing administration, Éamon de Valera's name was first put before the Dáil for election as the new Taoiseach. When the deputies divided into the 'Tá' and 'Níl' lobbies, the Fianna Fáil leader's re-nomination as Taoiseach was defeated by seventy-five votes to seventy. Had three opposition deputies voted with Fianna Fáil the party would have remained in power. John A. Costello's name was then proposed. He was elected Taoiseach by seventy-five votes to sixty-eight. He had the support of Fine Gael, Clann na Poblachta, Clann na Talmhan, the two Labour groups and eight independent deputies. When the result was declared one deputy, Oliver Flanagan, said: 'Thanks be to God that I have lived to see this day' to which the Ceann Comhairle retorted: 'Order. Deputy Flanagan should not start off on the wrong foot so early in this new Dáil.'

The parties in the new government had a diverse range of ideologies and backgrounds. From the centre left to the left were Clann na Talmhan, the two Labour groups and the quasi-republican Clann na Poblachta. Fine Gael was positioned on the 'right' and seen as representing business, large farmers and so-called 'commonwealth' interests. It is fair to say that Fine Gael was conservative and had a middle-class appeal, characteristics exemplified by its former vice-president and future leader James Dillon. He had resigned from Fine Gael in 1941 over the party's position on neutrality although he was still close to senior figures in the party. As Minister for Agriculture, Dillon's role was in part to be the representative in the cabinet of the independent deputies.

The new government sought to offer a credible alternative

to Fianna Fáil. However, as subsequent events would clearly illustrate, the grouping was a product of pragmatic political necessity rather than of coherent political theory. There was no real programme for government. In reality, the new government was a very loose coalition arrangement with several distinctive elements.

On the day the inter-party government was elected, Seán Lemass attempted to highlight some of its weak spots. As he saw it these started from its use of the term 'inter-party' rather than 'coalition'. Lemass asked Costello what the difference between the two concepts was and if 'inter-party' meant that collective responsibility did not apply? Costello did not take the bait offered by Lemass, merely replying that he did 'not care whether Deputy Lemass calls this a coalition, an inter-party government, or anything else. He can call it what he likes. A group of parties has come together and found agreement. That is an experiment, if you like.' Brian Farrell has observed: 'It is a measure of Fianna Fáil success in denouncing the concept of coalition that the combination chose to describe itself as "the inter-party government".'

The 1948 inter-party government also involved a marked shift in the relationship between the Taoiseach and his cabinet. In the first instance, Costello lacked the authority which comes with being party leader. Nor did he have any choice in the selection of ministers. The allocation of ministerial positions was determined by the parliamentary arithmetic of the different parties in the government. The choice of who filled these ministerial positions was then left to the individual parties. It is believed that Seán MacBride had a large say in the composition of the cabinet. He knew in advance of, and favoured, Patrick McGilligan's appointment as Minister for Finance. McGilligan was Fine Gael deputy for Dublin North-East and had considerable ministerial experience. He had been part of the Cumann na nGaedhael administrations from 1924 to 1932 and had held the portfolio of Industry and Commerce as well as External Affairs from 1927.

The Clann leader himself took the position of External Affairs. The second cabinet position which Clann occupied was given by MacBride to one of his party's newest political recruits - Dr Noël Browne. This appointment was seen as a measure to allay Fine Gael fears of a strongly republican Clann presence at the cabinet table. It was also a recognition of the section of the party which had brought much of Clann's electoral success in the general election. Maurice Manning has observed: 'The party was to supply the two most controversial members of that cabinet.' Seán MacBride later said he appointed Browne 'because he had no associations with the past, and I felt it was necessary to get somebody new who would have a fresh approach to problems'.

As well as losing power over ministerial selection, Costello also lost his constitutional right to nominate eleven members to Seanad Éireann. MacBride had a say in the appointment of two of the Taoiseach's eleven Seanad nominees. Denis Ireland was a Northern Protestant while Dr Patrick McCartan had unsuccessfully contested the 1945 presidential election as an independent candidate. He was one of the losing

Clann candidates in the 1948 general election.

Denis Ireland was a journalist and shared MacBride's views on monetary matters. He first spoke in the Seanad in June 1948, declaring that he would 'approach every piece of legislation in this Chamber from the point of view of the reunification of our country as a primary objective of Irish politics'. He described himself as a Protestant republican committed to ' . . . demolishing the unnatural border between the two parts of the country'. During his three years as a member of the Seanad, Denis Ireland's contributions for the most part made reference to partition, although in October 1949 he did introduce a motion calling for the reform of the country's monetary policy. Seán MacBride replied for the government, taking the opportunity to outline Clann views on the subject. In truth neither Ireland nor McCartan used their positions to advance the cause of the party that nominated them to the Seanad.

The decisions taken by the Clann leader to appoint Browne to the cabinet and to nominate these two senators were very dubious. They did nothing for party loyalty and served only to upset and disappoint people. Years later MacBride admitted that he was criticised within Clann for these decisions. The appointment of Noël Browne rubbed some of the old guard up the wrong way. It is understood that several senior members, including Lehane and Breathnach, were opposed to Browne's appointment. Peadar Cowan had seen himself as Minister for Defence. Noel Hartnett is believed to have been upset at having been overlooked for one of the Seanad seats. Hartnett was disappointed not to have won a Dáil seat. He had been one of the driving forces behind Clann's electoral campaign, using the experience he had gained as a member of Fianna Fáil to the benefit of the new party. MacBride and Harnett had been close associates prior to the formation of the inter-party government. The subsequent distancing in their relationship was a loss to Clann.

Con Lehane later expressed his belief that Clann was wrong to enter government and that the introduction of so-called 'intellectuals of the left', such as Hartnett and Browne, diluted the party's republicanism and therefore its effectiveness. He was not alone in this thinking. Many of the republican elements within Clann were uneasy about the decision to enter government with Fine Gael. Instead of appeasing this republican constituency, MacBride widened the gulf within the party by his choice of Seanad and cabinet nominees.

It was only over time that it became evident that these were fatal blows to Clann's position. Having entered government the party's priority was to make that government work. One of the first changes made by the new administration was to exclude the secretary to the government from Cabinet meetings, a decision taken at Seán MacBride's request. This was the first time since the foundation of the state that there was no member of the cabinet secretariat present at cabinet meetings. The Clann leader was worried about whether he could trust civil servants who had acted for Fianna Fáil for so many years. For this reason he requested that the Secretary of the Department of the

Taoiseach, who was also Secretary to the Government, should not be privy to the new cabinet's discussions. Instead the chief whip, future Taoiseach Liam Cosgrave, took notes at the meeting. Subsequent minutes and decisions were then drafted and circulated by the cabinet secretariat in the usual way.

It has been argued that this departure from normal procedure weakened the government and contributed to the breakdown in communication which was to become a feature of its last days in office. The fact that not all decisions were fully and accurately recorded was a factor in the Mother and Child controversy. It is noticeable that in the second inter-party administration, Costello insisted that the Secretary to the Government attend cabinet meetings and minute all decisions.

Over the previous sixteen years, de Valera's Fianna Fáil had acted as a tightly controlled and cohesive collective with a united public face. Fianna Fáil ministers had confined their public statements to their own departmental responsibilities. Broader policy statements were left to the Taoiseach. Internal disputes rarely came to light outside the cabinet. Basil Chubb has noted it was 'to be expected that the exigencies of coalition would cause a loosening of the rather strict conventions which had been followed hitherto. In practice, however, changes were few.' In many instances, the cabinet secretariat resisted any attempted deviation from the established pattern. One example was when the secretariat sought to prevent the circulation of a memorandum from Seán MacBride which reiterated views expressed on an issue already decided by the cabinet. The Taoiseach acted on this on civil service advice.

Things were not, however, always so clear-cut. Some reduction in collective discipline during the initial stages of the inter-party government was to be expected, especially given the inexperience of many ministers. There was certainly laxer discipline than in the previous administration. Several ministers and backbenchers from the different parties made speeches outside the Dáil which trespassed on the responsibilities of colleagues. At times these revealed significant policy disagreements between the different elements in the government. Costello acted as a chairman at cabinet and largely succeeded in holding the government together in a collective manner. Seán MacBride, however, was determined to extend his influence and the influence of his party over the whole range of government policies.

Although he held the External Affairs portfolio, the Clann leader was to exert considerable impact over the government's economic policy. There were a number of reasons why MacBride had such a large say in a policy area which was obviously outside his own brief. In the first instance, as party leader, MacBride took it upon himself to watch developments in all policy areas. This was especially crucial in relation to policy emanating from the Department of Finance, given its central importance over the allocation and control of expenditure. It was important to monitor Finance if the policies Clann espoused, such as Browne's hospital building programme, were to be implemented. In addition, an economic committee of the cabinet was set up at MacBride's initiative. This was to play a significant role in the formation of economic policy throughout the life of the government. Basil Chubb has written that such committees were perhaps evidence of the need for the government to have 'devices to deal with lack of accord, actual or potential'.

The changing focus of the brief in the Department of External Affairs saw that department increasingly taking on economic responsibilities. The reality was that whoever held this portfolio was going to be drawn into economic policy areas. However, it is doubtful if anybody other than Seán MacBride would have taken on board to such an extent the possibilities presented by this new role.

Even before the change of government, External Affairs had begun to extend its range of activities and areas of influence. In his history of the Department of Finance, Ronan Fanning notes that its archives reveal an 'explosive growth' in the volume of its records from 1946-47 onwards, especially documentation from the Department of External Affairs. He argues that MacBride's appointment 'as a strong, independently-minded and outward-looking minister powerfully reinforced tendencies which were already apparent in External Affairs . . . '

The Clann leader was advised by a small group consisting of Bulmer Hobson, Berthon Waters and Father Edward Cahill. Their thinking had influenced the economic policies which Clann had put forward in the preceding general election. Indeed, Bulmer Hobson and Berthon Waters were among those whom MacBride continued to consult on economic and financial policy throughout his years in public life. Waters was to write many long memoranda for MacBride at the Clann leader's request. These advisers had been influenced by the papal encyclicals of the 1930s and the social policy advocated by the Roman Catholic Bishop of Clonfert. It has been argued by Peter Mair that Clann members were 'at pains to demonstrate their adherence to prevailing Catholic teaching' in their policy and electoral statements. At the beginning of one of its publications the party stated that 'the structure of the Christian state is based on the family. Sociologically and morally the family is essential to the nation'.

These advisers were totally opposed to continuing the link with sterling as well as to the establishment of a central bank in the form proposed in the majority report of the Banking Commission. This report had been published a number of years earlier and was very much in keeping with the received wisdom of officials of the Department of Finance. Indeed, MacBride's advisers were responsible for drafting what became the minority report of that Commission.

The value of the Irish currency in 1948 was still linked to sterling. In effect this meant that policy over the Irish pound was determined by the British authorities. The state's assets were to a large extent invested in London. Relations between officials in the Department of Finance and the British Treasury were good. In his book on the period, Ronan Fanning notes that these relations were 'aptly symbolised by the existence of a direct telephone link between Finance and the Treasury, not only throughout the

1922–39 period but for much of the war . . . '

MacBride's advisers were not convinced there was need for such a close relationship. They believed that senior officials of the Department of Finance believed that it was not the responsibility of government to secure and maintain full employment. They were of the view that the stance adopted by officials in Finance was based on the assumption that the future economic history of Ireland was to be a continuation of past and present trends. Indeed, the Department of Finance strongly believed the link with sterling was in the best interests of the Irish economy. This was based on the extent of Irish trade with the UK and the amount of Irish foreign investments held in sterling. The views expressed by MacBride's advisers were opposed by officials in Finance who saw Clann policy as a deterrent to enterprise and, if implemented, as having the potential to shake public confidence in the Irish currency, in the banking system and even in the solvency of the state.

Officials in the Department of Finance had been worried about the policies that might be adopted by the inter-party government, in particular the policies advocated by Clann na Poblachta. These concerns were aroused when, as one of his first actions after his by-election victory, Seán MacBride put down a series of questions in the Dáil on the currency issue.

Economics was to play a much bigger role in political life after 1945. New theories propounded by John Maynard Keynes were feeding into mainstream political thought in Britain. The intervention of government in economic life, which Keynes advocated, was taken up with gusto by the new Labour government in the UK. In Ireland, it was to be some time before Keynesian thought entered the language of politicians but the policy of Clann na Poblachta did call for greater state intervention to boost economic activity and generate jobs. In the corridors of the Department of Finance such a stance was still rejected as too dangerous. Divisions over how the economy should be run came to the fore not long after the inter-party government was elected.

The American government framed the Marshall Aid Programme to revitalise the European economy after the ending of the Second World War. Ireland's interests in the programme were handled by the Department of External Affairs, a factor which further extended the Department's reach into economic policy. Senior officials in the Department of Finance were highly sceptical of the benefits which might accrue to Ireland under the aid programme. In 1946 the Secretary of the Department had observed: 'We cannot expect any measure of salvation from the so-called Marshall Plan.' Finance officials were worried the aid programme would led to increased borrowings as well as jeopardising the special Anglo-Irish financial relationship.

Seán MacBride had responsibility for drafting the Irish programme to qualify for Marshall Aid, the Irish European Recovery Programme. His influence was further enhanced by his friendship with the American Ambassador to Ireland, George Garrett. It has been said they regularly shared a lunch of poached eggs on toast in MacBride's office in Iveagh House. MacBride hoped Ireland would receive $150 million from the Marshall Aid programme. He was seeking the aid in the form of a grant rather then a loan, as it was claimed that Ireland would be unable to repay a loan. However, in the end a loan of £36 million was offered, far less than what had been anticipated.

These additional resources offered the possibility of funding a whole range of projects which otherwise would have remained on the drawing-board. MacBride believed this money would 'transform our country'. The Clann leader took the view that the funds must be used for economic development, that is by implementing policies such as those favoured by Clann na Poblachta, including land reclamation and afforestation. MacBride took the precaution of discussing his afforestation proposals with both Costello and McGilligan before publicising them – and before Finance officials got wind of them.

Around this time, an official in the Department of Finance, T. K. Whitaker, wrote that:

> land reclamation, drainage and afforestation, though like many other things desirable in themselves, fall far short of yielding an adequate revenue to offset the corresponding debt service . . . Expansionist ideas, however admirable, which involve adding to the public debt and to future taxation are completely out of touch with the reality of the present financial position.

Clann, however, believed these investments would ultimately yield returns to the Exchequer well in excess of the initial capital injection.

Not everyone in Clann was happy with the Marshall Aid programme. Peadar Cowan spoke in the Dáil on 1 July, and his views were 'somewhat different' from his colleagues. While the Dublin North-East deputy said that the 'American government are to be admired for their generosity to Europe' he believed the aid programme was a way 'to promote the foreign policy of the United States . . . ' Cowan described the aid programme, negotiated by his party leader, as 'a surrender of certain of our national rights'. MacBride and Cowan had exchanges in the Dáil chamber on Cowan's interpretation of the aid programme.

This embarrassing situation not only illustrated the lack of control within Clann but also was to give a fatal blow to Cowan's membership of the party. The following day the National Executive of Clann met. Forty members voted on an expulsion motion proposed by MacBride and seconded by Senator Patrick McCartan. The resolution was carried by thirty-five votes to five. A statement was issued after the meeting. It noted that ' . . . Captain Cowan, TD, was expelled from Clann na Poblachta for disloyalty to the organisation and was requested to resign his Dáil seat.' Cowan described the expulsion as 'harsh and unjustifiable'. He told the *Irish Times* that his local constituency organisation understood it was an 'attempt by certain individuals in Clann na Poblachta to make a "yes-man" of me and that I resisted it.'

Cowan also revealed that he had attended a meeting of the party's parliamentary party the day before his Dáil speech. He had hoped to discuss the Marshall Aid Programme at that meeting but MacBride was not present. Neither, it turns out, were the Health Minister Noël Browne nor Con Lehane, who Cowan described as the deputy leader of the party. Cowan noted that in view of their absence from the parliamentary party meeting no decision was taken on Clann policy on the aid programme. Consequently he believed he was at liberty to adopt the line he took in the Dáil debate. Given MacBride's central role in negotiating the aid programme it was somewhat naïve of Cowan to believe the Clann leader would have tolerated opposition to it within his party. But the non-attendance of key Clann members at the parliamentary party meeting typifies the lax attitude which had been adopted towards Clann structures.

Cowan did not resign his seat and remained an independent deputy. He said he would continue to press for the achievement of the aims, objectives and ideals of Clann. When asked if he would continue to support the inter-party government he replied, 'I am not committing myself.' By the end of July he had crossed the Dáil floor to vote with the Opposition. He continued his prolific output in the Dáil, making contributions on a vast array of issues. During the debate on the agriculture estimates he engaged in banter with Agriculture Minister, James Dillon. At one stage Cowan described himself ' . . . as a deputy who has been cast into the wilderness in the last few days'. Over the remainder of the lifetime of the inter-party government, Cowan in general remained a supporter of the government but his support could never be counted on and on a number of occasions he voted against it.

The inter-party government pressed on after the Cowan affair. The 1946 census for the first time contained evidence about the availability of water supplies and sanitation in households throughout the country. The results clearly indicated that facilities now regarded as basic, such as lighting, water supply and sanitation, were totally absent in many homes around the country. Only one in five of all houses had piped water while three-quarters of farm dwellings were without an indoor toilet. The housing stock was very badly run down. Against this background the government attempted with the help of Marshall Aid to improve the depressed state of the economy and the living standards of the Irish people.

Historian John A. Murphy has argued that 'the beginnings of economic planning are to be found in this first coalition period, predating by seven years T. K. Whitaker's famous memo . . . which is still popularly believed to be the point of departure for government economic programming'. The government published a long-term recovery programme in the form of a White Paper in January 1949. The responsibility for producing the White Paper rested with the Department of External Affairs. T. K. Whitaker, who was involved in preparing the recovery programme, saw it 'as an exercise that had to be undertaken to persuade the Americans to give us Marshall Aid'. Ronan Fanning's less severe assessment is that:

It does illustrate how, after 1948, ministers
and government officials alike became increasingly concerned with framing a longer-
term financial and economic policy than had
previously been contemplated. The days of ad
hoc, year-to-year, financial management were
clearly numbered.

According to *The Economist* magazine, the 1950 budget
introduced by the inter-party government 'provided an
innovation in Irish public finance by a formal division
between capital and current expenditure'. This was the
country's first separate capital budget. Patrick Lynch, who
acted as an economic adviser to the Taoiseach, described it
as 'the first explicit expression of Keynes in an Irish budget'.
Current government expenditure in that year was budgeted
for £75.7 million. The total taxation take was put at about
23 per cent of national income, estimated at being around
£350 million in 1949 compared with £335 million the
previous year and £154 million in 1938. The decision to
introduce a capital budget had been signalled by the Taoiseach
at the end of the previous year and had government support
including that of the Minister for Finance, Patrick McGilligan.
Ronan Fanning claims the latter 'was one of the earliest of
Keynes's converts among Irish politicians'. McGilligan was in
fact one of the linchpins of the government and although
less radical than Clann would have wished, he was not
completely subject to the advice of his officials in the
Department of Finance.

There were times when MacBride's utterances were contrary to statements from, and stances adopted by, the Finance Minister. The opposition party was not, however, going to be allowed to score political points. McGilligan told the Dáil:

> Deputies on the other side of the House have anguished themselves with talk about the public embarrassment which there is over the fact that the Minister for External Affairs does not talk the same financial language as myself. I have yet to meet anybody outside the ranks of the professional politicians who is worried about that. Nobody is worried. Have we got to the stage when, on a matter which may be an important point of policy when it is decided, we cannot have freedom of speech? Have we go to the stage when men, just because they join the government circle, must all, as one deputy said, when they go out of the council chambers, speak the same language?

While MacBride was busy in External Affairs, his party colleague in cabinet set about implementing changes in the Department of Health. Browne's objectives were to make progress on general health issues, a hospital building programme and tackling tuberculosis. In his own words he was determined 'to revolutionise the quality of the health services'. As a doctor, Browne was well qualified for the ministerial post he had been given. He had first-hand experience of TB and had worked as a medical officer in sanatoria in England and at home. Without doubt the virtual eradication of tuberculosis from Ireland is his legacy. The funding for his massive hospital building programme was provided by the Hospital Sweepstakes Fund. In his autobiography, *Against the Tide*, Browne wrote that the programme 'had immediate results. By July 1950 2,000 beds had been provided for TB patients, bringing the total up to 5,500. The tuberculosis death rate dropped dramatically from 123 per 100,000 in 1947 to 73 per 100,000 in 1951.' In his time as Health Minister, Browne also established the National Blood Transfusion Organisation.

Officials in the Department of Finance were wary of such expenditure, which went against all the dogma which had guided economic policy over the previous three decades. They were worried that increased government expenditure would lead to a rise in inflation and a worsening of the balance of payments. The government also established the Industrial Development Authority and Córas Trachtála. The establishment of the former body was at the time vigorously opposed by Fianna Fáil. MacBride and his Clann colleagues, however, fully supported the new bodies. Indeed, Clann wanted to link the IDA to one of its own policy proposals. It believed that the state's external assets should be repatriated so as to provide the IDA with finance to build factories.

The fact that Ireland's external reserves were largely held in sterling meant that the Irish currency was put under pressure when sterling suffered due to the economic problems which affected the British government in those years. The sterling link was to develop into a crisis of sorts in 1949 when it became clear that sterling was going to be devalued. Clann presented the cabinet with what Ronan Fanning calls a 'formidable memorandum' on the inevitability of devaluation. It contained views which were totally different from those prevailing as conventional wisdom in the Department of Finance.

The remedy Clann proposed was that the government should take immediate and urgent action:

> as a matter of definite policy, [to] endeavour, by every means available, to promote the repatriation of our 'sterling assets' and the investment of moneys at present invested in Britain, in national development projects in Ireland. Such policy would serve the double purpose of safeguarding our 'sterling assets' and of preventing the effects of the depression. Any reasonable impartial objective view of the situation leaves no doubt that, putting it in the mildest form possible, there is a definite element of speculation in investing Irish moneys in Britain at a time the British economy and sterling are confronted with such dangers and uncertainties.

The Clann leader went on to argue that the Irish state should have invested the capital, which it had allocated to

British securities since 1914, in such projects as the creation of state forests, the Shannon scheme and the land rehabilitation scheme. He claimed that if such a policy had been followed, a 64 per cent depreciation in sterling assets between 1914 and 1948 would have been avoided and such 'invaluable assets' as a reduction in imports, an increase in employment and raw material for industry would have been acquired. MacBride saw his party's proposals as 'not merely anticipating the possibility of devaluation and depression but of remedying some of the basic defects present in our economy'. Clann urged that the question of maintaining the Irish pound at parity with sterling 'be examined as a matter of urgency by independent economists', suggesting that the evidence given in the Banking Commission's majority report 'if valid then, [is] not valid now'. The extent of the division between the views of Clann and those of Finance was clear for all with an insight into the workings of the government to see.

On the morning of Saturday 17 September 1949 senior officials in the Department of Finance finally received official news of the British decision to devalue the pound sterling. That evening the government met in emergency session in Iveagh House. The meeting continued until three o'clock the next morning and resumed on Sunday evening. The two Clann ministers, MacBride and Browne, argued strongly against the Irish government's devaluing with the British. One of the Finance officials present was T. K. Whitaker. He remembers the Clann leader sitting astride a chair in the middle of the room with other ministers sitting around the sides. MacBride was, according to Whitaker, relentlessly cross-examining senior Finance officials. Whitaker believed that MacBride intended to question all officials present and that this would expose major inconsistencies in their opinions, particularly regarding the probable effect of devaluation on the cost of living. In the end the Clann position was not accepted; the government decided on an equivalent devaluation of the Irish pound in line with that agreed for sterling by their British counterparts.

Two days later several departments, including External Affairs, were asked to submit memoranda on 'the effects of devaluation and the further steps that it may necessitate'. A considerable proportion of the memorandum from the Department of External Affairs was given over to criticism of the advice provided by the Department of Finance and the Central Bank throughout the devaluation crisis. The following month Seán MacBride delivered a series of lectures and talks, some on the radio and some to Clann meetings. These were later published under the title *Our People, Our Money*. The Governor of the Central Bank, Joseph Brennan, felt that one of those lectures amounted to 'a public censure of the Central Bank' and he made his annoyance known to the Taoiseach and Minister for Finance.

The fall-out from the devaluation controversy was later responsible for Clann's taking the 'strongest exception' to Brennan's reappointment as the Governor of the Central Bank in 1950. The Clann leader objected to Brennan on the grounds that his 'views, policy and acts . . . are in direct conflict with the policy of the government'. He argued that in an inter-party government the position should be filled by an agreed nominee and wrote to Costello to this effect in a letter dated 30 January 1950. Yet despite Clann's objections, Brennan was reappointed for a further term.

Much has been made of the decision to appoint Browne to cabinet. His comparative youth and inexperience are often highlighted. But in assuming responsibility for External Affairs, Seán MacBride was taking on one of the toughest jobs in government. Not only had he to look after the interests of his party but he was taking a job which had previously been held by the Fianna Fáil leader. Éamon de Valera had had total control over Irish foreign policy since 1932 in his dual capacity as head of government and Minister for External Affairs. In addition, James Dillon was recognised as one of the most able speakers on foreign affairs in Dáil Éireann. Thus, from day one, MacBride was under the spotlight. If there were any slips, comparisons would inevitably be made. It is a mark of his ability that when he left office many of the tributes which were paid make reference to him as the best minister to have served in that department. One of the negative consequences of such a demanding portfolio was that there was less time to attend to the needs of the fledging political party he led.

The first electoral test of the new government was the local elections in Kerry and Dublin in mid-1948. The remainder of the local council elections did not take place until 1950. Clann had performed respectably in the two Kerry constituencies in the general election. Although the party had failed to win a seat in either the Kerry North or

Kerry South constituencies it polled well in both. John Connor led the way in the Tralee electoral area. A farmer, he had received over four thousand first preferences in the general election. In the local contest Connor polled over seven hundred votes, finishing second only to Labour's Dan Spring, father of the future Tánaiste. He was to stay loyal to Clann until his tragic death in 1956. The party also took seats in Listowel, Killarney and Killorglin. The three councillors elected in these electoral areas had not contested the general election. John O'Leary, a chemist's assistant from Killarney, stood unsuccessfully for election to the Dáil in the following two general elections.

For Dublin County Council Clann put forward eleven candidates and won two seats. Few of the unsuccessful candidates from the 1948 general election ran in these local elections. It was to tell against them later in that none of the party's Dáil deputies used the elections as an opportunity to consolidate their local bases.

In mid-December Con Lehane took the opportunity during a Dáil debate of addressing the government's performance in its first ten months in office. He made no reference to Clann's performance in the recent local elections but said that he took 'a particular pride in the achievements of our two ministers'. The Clann Deputy Leader praised the Minister for Local Government but suggested to James Dillon, the Minister for Agriculture, 'that a little less volatility and a little less flamboyance might serve him better in the conduct of his Department'. Fianna Fáil deputies had been suggesting that Fine Gael, Clann na Talmhan and

Clann na Poblachta might merge but Lehane said such suggestions were 'no more based on fact than the other fairy tales of Herr Hans Andersen'.

Officials in the Department of Finance would have been horrified by Lehane's views on the economy. From his comments it is clear that Keynesian economics was beginning to enter the language and thought of some Irish politicians. Contrary to the economic conservatism preached by Finance, Lehane said the government 'must realise that one of its primary duties is to provide employment for our people at home'. He argued: 'it is only by wise spending that increased production and increased employment can combat the twin evils of emigration and unemployment'. The Dublin South-Central deputy said that Clann 'did not believe in retrenchment for retrenchment's sake', an obvious reference to the views of the Department of Finance. He made reference to government initiation of schemes for land reclamation, drainage, housing and afforestation adding: 'if the day comes when we are convinced that they cannot produce those results we shall be quite prepared then to put this government out'.

Peadar Cowan, who had spent six of the government's first ten months outside the Clann fold, also took a less positive view of its early endeavours. He argued that members of the cabinet were 'not so much part of a team as individuals working in watertight compartments, interfering not at all with the work of the other departments or ministers'. Cowan continued: 'There is not that coordination of effort, co-ordination of policy, coordination of programme that is essential if we are to solve all those very serious problems which confront us.' The now independent deputy noted that 'the normal lifetime of this parliament is five years, and if the other four years go as quickly and in the same way as this present year has gone I am afraid that we will have very little to show for our efforts . . . '

The majority of local authorities held elections in 1950. Clann's approach to the 1950 local elections was outlined under eight headings which included roads, education, drainage, afforestation, housing and public health. The party promised to create a clean and efficient administration and to cooperate with all parties in the formation of a progressive policy to the benefit of all. These vague aspirations were accompanied by a number of specific proposals. As in the 1948 general election, Clann wanted to see the provision of extra scholarships to give better opportunity 'to the poor man's child'. Interestingly in light of subsequent events the party's 1950 local election 'approach to local government' included a commitment for the 'provision of the best medical treatment for everyone in need of it, irrespective of his or her ability to pay'. Fianna Fáil attacked Clann's participation in the inter-party government. Major Vivion de Valera said that 'for the sake of two minority cabinet seats, they, like Labour, had sacrificed their prospects and supporters'. This does not seem to have been an issue with the electorate; many local newspapers noted the public's lack of enthusiasm for the elections.

Despite this lack of enthusiasm, the 1950 local elections provided Clann with an opportunity to establish a substantial local base throughout the country. The lack of such a base was one of its weaknesses in the previous general election. By now Tom Roycroft was General Secretary of the party. He would have been aware that by getting local councillors elected the party was grooming potential Dáil candidates. This was the second big problem which bedevilled Clann in 1948. Michael Gallagher has noted that ' . . . no candidate, especially in a rural constituency, can expect to be elected unless he has an extensive network of local contacts and a strong local base'. In essence, local elections are an ideal platform from which to launch future Dáil candidates.

Clann appears, however, to have had difficulty in getting candidates to stand for election. There were no Clann candidates in four council areas: Carlow, Kildare, Offaly and Waterford County Council. This would seem to indicate the poor condition of the party's organisational structures. It appears that little effort had been made following the 1948 general election to plan for subsequent electoral contests. Without such planning and structures, the likelihood of Clann ever attaining its objective of replacing Fianna Fáil remained little more than an objective. The party had 159 candidates. In the end only twenty-six of these were elected. In a number of areas Clann failed to make any impression. Despite running candidates, it won no seats in Cork City Borough, Laois, Louth, Meath, Wexford, Wicklow or Sligo. These failures in effect ended Clann's presence in most of these constituencies. Only in the latter three did the party again put forward candidates at Dáil elections.

Many of those who won local council seats had been

unsuccessful Dáil candidates in 1948. This at least indicates some degree of continuity for the party. However, the vast majority of those who stood in 1948 were never again to contest an election for Clann. What the results indicate is the beginning of a consolidation of Clann interests on a number of specific individuals in specific constituencies.

Clann put forward sixteen candidates for seats on Dublin City Council. They won only two seats on the council to add to the two Clann councillors elected to the county council two years previously. The party therefore had four local authority councillors in Dublin, whereas six Clann Dáil deputies had been elected for the same region in the 1948 general election. Joseph Barron took a council seat, joined by newcomer Michael Ffrench O'Carroll. Barron was to contest five subsequent general elections for the party, finally taking a Dáil seat in Dublin South-Central in 1961.

Clann took a single seat on Donegal County Council. Hugh Duggan from Glenties had been unsuccessful in the 1948 general election in Donegal West. Although he did not contest the by-election in the constituency in 1949, he ran for Clann in the 1950 local elections, polling only three votes less than the sitting Fianna Fáil TD Cormac Breslin. However, he did not fight any further elections for the Clann. The candidate in the 1949 by-election, Alphonsus Canning, ran in the Donegal electoral area in the 1950 local elections. Although he polled over one thousand first preferences he did not take a seat. The 1950 local elections saw the last electoral presence for Clann in County Donegal.

Another failed general election candidate took a council

seat in Galway. Out of sixteen candidates Clann managed to get one elected to Galway County Council. Vincent Shields was elected to the Council from the Loughrea Electoral Area. He ran unsuccessfully in three subsequent Dáil elections for the party.

In Clare, Clann nominated nine candidates; three were elected. Two of the three candidates in the previous general election went forward. Both Tim Smythe from Ennis and Kilkee-based Thomas Lillis were elected along with assurance representative Seán O'Connor from Miltown Malbay. The third candidate in Clare in the 1948 general election was Peter O'Loughlin, who polled the highest of the three Clann candidates. In the intervening period he parted ways with Clann and contested the 1950 locals as an independent. Again he was defeated. Tim Smythe noted that the future for Clann was now bright. He added that when the party's policy had first been put before the electorate there were certain misrepresentations and that the public had been misled into not accepting it.

Eight candidates went forward for Clann in Leitrim. Michael McGovern from Manorhamilton was the only one elected. He stood in the Sligo-Leitrim constituency in the 1951 and 1954 general elections. But polling less than 7 per cent of the first preference vote on both occasions, he never came near winning a Dáil seat.

The two Clann candidates elected to Mayo County Council had been unsuccessful general election candidates in 1948. Martin McGrath had lost out in Mayo North, while Owen Hughes was defeated in the Mayo South constituency. Both stood in the 1950 locals and were elected. McGrath, who was from Ballina, used his position to build a base to contest three subsequent Dáil elections. At a by-election in 1952 he polled almost one-fifth of the first-preference vote in Mayo North although he did not take the seat. His vote in 1954, the last general election in which he ran, was substantially down on this figure. Owen Hughes, who was elected to the county council for the Westport area, appears not to have followed up this success.

The Clones and Castleblaney electoral areas between them returned two Clann councillors to Monaghan County Council. Despite this success Clann did not contest the constituency in the following general election. A defeated Clann candidate in the 1950 local elections went on to stand for the party in the 1954 general election although without any success.

In Westmeath none of the party's six candidates in the 1950 local elections had run in the previous general election. Only one of these newcomers, Gerard Jennings from Mullingar, was elected to the county council. He was one of three candidates the party nominated in the Longford-Westmeath constituency at the following general election although none were successful.

Roscommon was Jack McQuillan's constituency. The young Dáil deputy was joined on the local county council by three Clann colleagues. McQuillan topped the poll in his own electoral area and managed to bring in another Clann representative, thereby consolidating his strong position in the constituency. With four elected councillors, Roscommon joined Kerry County Council as having the most Clann members. In Roscommon the defeated Clann candidates in the 1950 local elections went on to stand for the party at subsequent Dáil elections, John Scott in 1954 and Peter McGuinness in 1961. However, after McQuillan's split with Clann in 1951 the party lost its position in Roscommon and never looked like building on the successes of the first few years.

In Kilkenny, republican Patrick Gleeson, who stood unsuccessfully for Clann in the 1948 general election, was elected to the county council.

Stephen Coughlan was treasurer of the party organisation in Limerick East in 1948. He was one of seven candidates in the 1950 local elections in Limerick City. Along with Ted Russell, Coughlan was elected to the city council. Russell, a Clann candidate in the 1948 general election, had been elected at the previous local elections as an independent candidate. He got 952 first-preference votes and took one of the aldermanships on the new council. When the new council came to vote in a mayor, there was a tie between Russell and the Fianna Fáil nominee. The two names were placed in a hat but Russell lost – although his time was to come several years later. Clann also had one councillor elected to Limerick County Council.

In Leitrim Clann put up five candidates. Martin McGowan, a teacher from Manorhamilton, attempted to maximise on the positive contribution Browne was making in the Department of Health. He told the electorate that the party was 'carrying out a war against disease'. None of Clann's three candidates in the 1948 general election contested the local elections in this area. Republican veteran John Leonard from Tubbercurry had been elected to Leitrim County Council in 1942 but changed allegiance when Clann was formed. However, he did not stand again for public office.

Two of Clann's nine candidates were elected to Tipperary North Riding County Council. Michael Cronin had been Patrick Kinnane's running mate in the 1948 general election, a role he again played in the 1954 general election. The second Clann councillor, Daniel Kennedy, was to take up the mantle for Clann in the 1957 general election. In the Tipperary South council, as in other electoral areas, the sole success for Clann was one of its failed 1948 general election candidates. Denis O'Driscoll won a seat for the Fethard electoral area.

With twenty-six councillors to add to the number elected in Dublin and Kerry in 1949, Clann had the makings of an organisational structure – of sorts. The 1950 local elections had allowed members to consolidate their links with the fledgling party. The priority at this point was the extraction of maximum credit for Clann na Poblachta from its role in government. This in turn would have to be translated into greater electoral gains.

5

ACHIEVEMENTS, CONFLICTS AND SPLITS

Although the government gave Clann respectability, Fianna Fáil was still endeavouring to cast a slur on the true intentions of the party. The communist scare had partly worked in the 1948 general election and Fianna Fáil continued to raise the issue at every opportunity. In early 1949, while he was in America, Seán MacBride was asked about communist activity in Ireland. He replied that there were no communists in Ireland. This statement was picked up by Fianna Fáil and raised by Deputy Harry Colley in the Dáil. He pressed the Clann leader on whether or not the statement was based on official information. When MacBride said his statement was not based on official information, the Fianna Fáil deputy continued to press, in an obvious attempt to embarrass the Minister for External Affairs. MacBride conceded that he 'spoke officially' but that he 'did not speak from official information'. Seán Lemass described this statement as 'a typical lawyer's reply'. This was a comment to which MacBride took objection:

I beg your pardon. Now that you have asked for an explanation you will get it. I was asked at a press interview whether it was true that there was a strong Communist Party here. I said there was no Communist Party in this portion of Ireland. No doubt, as a result of some of the misrepresentations made by some of the deputy's colleagues, false impressions got abroad in some countries . . . I am aware of several statements which were made by deputy MacEntee.

Fianna Fáil deputies continued to dwell on the issue, raising statements from the Bishop of Cork in relation to the existence of a communist cell in that city. The Clann leader returned to his seat and did not reply any further.

The level of Dáil activity of the Clann deputies who were not at cabinet was very varied. Some ranged across all areas of government activity while others confined their contributions to issues concerning their own constituencies. Con Lehane and Peadar Cowan had impressive records for speaking in the House and asking questions on a whole variety of subjects. In one instance, prior to his expulsion from Clann, Peadar Cowan pressed the Taoiseach for a decision on the removal of a statue of Queen Victoria, 'a foreign monarch, from the Quadrangle at Leinster House'. He made a large number of contributions on a wide range of topics such as teachers' salaries and the need to set primary certificate examinations in Ulster Irish for children from Ulster counties. Con Lehane placed a number of parliamentary questions on issues such as the possibility of changing the names of streets in memory of people who gave service to the nation.

Other Clann deputies like Michael Fitzpatrick, Patrick Kinnane and John Tully only made a small number of contributions in the Dáil chamber. As he had done following his by-election victory, Kinnane kept his contributions to matters pertaining to his own constituency, such as the water supply and sewage scheme for Upperchurch in Thurles. Joseph Brennan also stayed mainly with constituency issues, asking questions about corporation housing in Dun Laoghaire and dredging Dalkey harbour. Overall an examination of the contributions of the Clann TDs illustrates the dual constituency which Clann represented. Issues such as housing and hospital provision were raised repeatedly, as were matters pertaining to the North.

Both Clann ministers are credited with organising their respective departments to meet the challenges which were to come in the year after they themselves had left office. In External Affairs, MacBride increased staffing and instigated a period of administrative reorganisation. Just as Browne will be remembered for his hospital programme and the eradication of TB, MacBride's name will be closely associated with the decision to repeal the External Relations Act.

There was little coordination between the two Clann ministers. In his autobiography, Browne has written that he 'soon formed the conclusion that the important decisions which we debated in Cabinet had already been determined elsewhere . . . Seán MacBride was accepted by my colleagues as the senior spokesman of the two of us'. Nevertheless, it is interesting to note that when MacBride was absent it was Browne who substituted for him, in effect as the acting Minister for External Affairs.

Given his background and that of his party, it was inevitable that Seán MacBride would bring a republican outlook to government. The ending of partition and a formalising of the state's relationship with the United Kingdom were two of the aims of Clann na Poblachta. Ireland's relationship with the Commonwealth was to a large extent ambiguous. While Britain still considered Ireland a member, Éamon de Valera had propounded the view that Ireland was a state outside the Commonwealth while at the same time having some form of external relationship with it.

There were some fears that Clann would embark on a hard-line republican agenda when in government but Seán MacBride appears to have been realistic about what could be achieved in these areas. While the North had been a frequent topic for all Clann speakers in the 1948 general election, throughout the campaign MacBride had placed equal importance on the need for economic development. Many of the party's more republican candidates had been defeated in the polling booths. So while Clann was still a 'darker shade of green' than the other parties, after the 1948 general election the republican component of the party was matched in numbers and strength by those, like Noël Browne, with a social agenda.

The primary domestic and foreign policy objective of the

state was not altered by the change of government. The ending of partition remained the policy objective which underpinned the Department of External Affairs. Under MacBride's direction the department became involved in a huge propaganda war on the partition issue, which, however, failed to win the country any real international support. If anything, the anti-partition campaign may have been counter-productive, merely serving to harden Unionist opinion in the North.

Yet the popular appeal which MacBride brought to the partition issue was of concern to Fianna Fáil. They were worried about Clann trumping them within the republican constituency both domestically and internationally. Indeed, not long after the inter-party government came to office, Éamon de Valera embarked on his own anti-partition drive. This involved the Fianna Fáil leader touring the United States to assure leading Irish-Americans that he was still the leader of Irish constitutional republicanism.

Ireland's neutrality during the Second World War cut the country off from the rest of the world. When the war ended contacts with the outside world were limited. Over the following few years the Department of External Affairs was responsible for extending Ireland's contacts and position with the international community. In July 1948, not long after coming into office, Seán MacBride told the Dáil: 'Our sympathies lie clearly with Western Europe' although 'the continuance of partition precludes us from taking our rightly [sic] place in the affairs of Europe'. Ireland was a founder member of the Council of Europe in 1949. The Council had a largely consultative role but it afforded the Clann leader an international stage of sorts to seek support for ending partition. At early meetings of the Council of Europe, the Irish government attempted to get the partition of the island on to the agenda but there was little support for the case being articulated by MacBride and his officials. One of the weaknesses of the stance adopted by MacBride was that it gave the world the impression that Ireland was not really interested in any other international policy areas except partition. When the second inter-party government came to power in 1956 it widened the brief of the country's foreign affairs policy.

Although many Clann members viewed partition as the number one issue, Seán MacBride was also serious about formalising the relationship with the United Kingdom. He was keen to ensure that other countries were fully aware of Ireland's independence. A story is told that when a new Argentinian ambassador appointed to Ireland arrived with his credentials addressed to King George VI, the Minister for External Affairs refused to accept them. He requested changes to their original form so that they were addressed to the Head of State as set down in the 1937 constitution. The papers were altered and addressed to the President, Seán T. O'Kelly. This was the first time an ambassador was presented to an Irish president.

On the day the inter-party government was voted in by the Dáil Seán MacBride made reference to the External Relations Act. He reiterated Clann's founding objective of 'the reintegration of this nation as a republic, free from any association with any other country'. MacBride, however, accepted the reality that Clann could not claim to have 'secured a mandate from the people that would enable us to repeal, or seek to repeal the External Relations Act and such other measures as are consistent with our status as an independent republic'.

There were other members of the inter-party government who shared the belief that the External Relations Act should be removed. Some were less pessimistic than MacBride about the possibility of the new government taking the necessary steps to have it repealed. One such minister was James Dillon. In a speech to the Dáil, also on the day the new government was voted into power, Dillon made reference to MacBride's comments. 'I observe that Deputy MacBride contemplates a long postponement of some objectives near his heart, but I am more optimistic than he.'

This was not one of the tasks which the inter-party government publicly set itself to achieve while in power but the issue was raised in the Dáil several months after it came into office. The Labour leader, Tánaiste William Norton, said that 'it would do our national self-respect good both at home and abroad if we were to proceed without delay to abolish the External Relations Act'. In the same Dáil debate, the Fianna Fáil leader Éamon de Valera acknowledged that if the government went on to repeal the act it would 'get no opposition' from his party.

There is conflicting evidence as to whether the issue was discussed at cabinet in the summer of 1948. However, with support from all sides in the Dáil it was no great surprise when it was announced that the government planned to repeal the act. It was the timing of the announcement that caused surprise. In September 1948, while in Canada, the Taoiseach held a news conference announcing his Government's intention to declare Ireland a republic. The news was to come as a surprise to many of Costello's cabinet colleagues. The Taoiseach had been informed of an article to be published in the *Sunday Independent* reporting on the Government's intentions. A telegram from MacBride advised Costello against any public response but the Taoiseach felt he would have no choice but to truthfully answer questions asked on the issue. It is also possible that Costello was fearful of someone like the former Clann deputy, Peadar Cowan, pre-empting the government through the introduction of a private members' motion.

The Republic of Ireland Bill was introduced in the Dáil in 24 November 1948. Most Clann Oireachtas members contributed to the debates on the 'Ireland Bill'. Joseph Brennan suggested making the day the Republic of Ireland Bill became law 'Independence Day' and a national holiday. His suggestion was never taken up. In the Seanad, Denis Ireland welcomed the Bill ' . . . as a Six-County Protestant Republican'. When the Bill was passed into law the following year, Ireland not only became a republic but left the Commonwealth. In making the announcement to repeal the Act the Taoiseach had stolen the limelight from his Minister for External Affairs. It was Costello who introduced the legislation repealing the External Relations Act and not MacBride as would have been expected. Indeed, Noël

Browne notes that 'MacBride, in a pitiful protest, did not appear at the Easter Sunday celebrations' when the Republic came into effect.

Along with the declaration of a Republic, the inter-party government is remembered for its attempts to introduce a comprehensive health scheme for mothers and children. Fine Gael had opposed the 1945 Public Health Bill proposed by the then Fianna Fáil government. It was considered to go against Catholic social teaching. When the Bill was reintroduced in 1947 the new Minister at the Department of Health, Dr James Ryan, adopted a more conciliatory approach. The main elements proposed included improving medical inspection in schools and provision of a non-means-tested free medical service for mothers and children up to the age of fourteen. At that time the main public opposition to the Bill was focused on the compulsory inspection of schoolchildren. James Dillon spoke against the Bill as it impinged on the rights of parents to have primary responsibility for their children's health.

At that time the Dáil was not aware of the protests made to Taoiseach Éamon de Valera by the country's Roman Catholic bishops. The Catholic hierarchy privately told de Valera:

> For the state, under the Act, to empower the public authority to provide for the health of all children, and to treat their ailments, and to educate women in regard to health, and to provide them with gynaecological services, was

> directly and entirely contrary to Catholic social
> teaching, the rights of the family, the rights of
> the Church in education, and the rights of the
> medical profession, and of voluntary institutions.

Members of the medical profession also had reservations about the financial implications of the proposals, which had the potential to limit their income from private practice.

The calling of the general election in early 1948 meant the legislation was put on hold and did not come up again until Noël Browne was appointed Minister for Health. This issue was eventually to lead to crisis in the inter-party government and turmoil in Clann na Poblachta, although it would be wrong to blame the government's collapse purely on the so-called 'Mother and Child' controversy. In fact this controversy merely brought to a head some of the differences which had been developing within Clann na Poblachta. In particular, it led to a bitter personal battle between Browne and MacBride.

There were rumblings at the start of 1951 that Clann was in trouble as a coherent political party. A final break had just occurred between MacBride and Noel Hartnett, who resigned over the so-called 'Baltinglass affair'. The Minister for Posts and Telegraphs, Jim Everett, became embroiled in controversy over the dismissal of the postmistress from the Baltinglass Post Office in his Wicklow constituency. She was replaced by a supporter of Everett. This caused widespread outrage, with protests throughout Wicklow and also outside the Dáil. Despite calls for his resignation, Everett refused to consider his position. The affair was finally resolved in early 1951 when the original postmistress was given her job back. Noel Hartnett claimed that Clann's acceptance of Everett's continued presence in government meant the party was now bereft of 'any political or social philosophy' and was obsessed with power.

Hartnett had become, as James Meehan puts it in his chapter on the economy in *Ireland in the War Years and After*, 'an invaluable bridge between the republican zealots and the social reformers' in Clann. Without doubt his resignation was a serious blow to the party. It was already a failure on the part of MacBride that he had not promoted Hartnett to a position in which his obvious organisational ability could have been used to Clann's benefit over the 1948 to 1951 period.

In late February the newspapers were reporting on divisions in Clann. Hartnett's resignation was only a precursor to more serious conflict. In 1950 Noël Browne decided to reintroduce elements of the Fianna Fáil Health Act. His proposals included free, but voluntary, ante- and post-natal care for mothers, along with free medical care for all children under the age of sixteen with no means test.

The Catholic bishops had reservations about Browne's scheme for the health services. On one hand they feared that mothers from their flock would receive care and instruction on issues like gynaecological hygiene from non-Catholic doctors. The members of the hierarchy were also in sympathy with the objections of the medical profession who worried about the introduction of 'socialised medicine'. This was shorthand for their fears over the loss of earnings from private practice. Significantly, one of the main opponents of the scheme, Archbishop John Charles McQuaid of Dublin, was the son of a doctor. After a meeting with some of the bishops in October 1950, the Minister for Health believed he had secured agreement to proceed with his scheme. However, this was not how the bishops saw it.

Professor Joe Lee has noted that 'had Browne not been so obdurate . . . a compromise might have been arranged' with the bishops. Browne proceeded with the scheme but continued disapproval from the Catholic Church and the medical profession eliminated any cabinet support for its introduction in the form Browne was proposing. Despite the obvious loss of support from cabinet colleagues, Browne was unwilling to see the health proposals defeated by pressure from the bishops and doctors. The stand-off continued during the early months of 1951 until the cabinet decided to drop the scheme following correspondence from the bishops. Browne recalls MacBride as saying: 'Those in the government who are Catholics are bound to accept the views of their Church.'

A meeting of the Clann National Executive was held on St Patrick's Day 1951. When Browne arrived at the meeting he heard a series of charges against him being read out. He challenged the authority of the meeting to discuss his behaviour or seek his expulsion from the party as neither were on the agenda. Browne then left the room despite pleas from people like McQuillan who wanted him to stay and defend himself. The divisions in Clann na Poblachta were soon to come fully into the open.

Browne met the bishops again to discuss the situation but no compromise was reached. Archbishop McQuaid wrote to the Taoiseach strongly suggesting that the Mother and Child Scheme as proposed should not proceed. There was a cabinet meeting the following day, 6 April. After months of going around in circles the government had decided to back the bishops. With this knowledge and the evidence of the recent Clann meeting, Browne knew his days as minister were almost over.

A special meeting of Clann's National Executive followed at three o'clock on Sunday 8 April. It was to last until four o'clock on Monday morning. Over these thirteen hours Seán MacBride took the opportunity to denounce his cabinet colleague for disloyalty. Browne was accused of being pro-Communist and anti-Catholic. In addition, MacBride alleged that Browne had his eyes on the leadership of Clann although Deputy Jack McQuillan later dismissed this claim as 'simply not in accordance with the facts'. Noël Browne has written that 'the cold venom of his (MacBride's) verbal assault on me still came as a shock'. The meeting ended with a vote of no confidence in Browne. All but three of the executive members voted in favour of MacBride's position. The Clann leadership was given the authority to seek the resignation of the Minister for Health.

Browne still had some hope that a compromise could be reached, and issued a press statement to the effect that he had deferred his decision on his future intentions. On 10 April 1951, Seán MacBride presented Noël Browne with a letter requesting his resignation as Minister for Health.

In that letter MacBride told Browne he would 'no doubt realise that, in light of the events that have happened, it would not now be possible for you to implement successfully the Mother and Child health service, which is urgently required and which the government and the Clann have undertaken to provide'. Interestingly MacBride went on to try to assure Browne that 'in reaching the decision that has compelled me to write this letter, I have sincerely sought to eliminate from my mind the other events, not connected with the Mother and Child services, which have rendered our collaboration increasingly difficult in the course of the last year'.

At the party's Árd Fheis the following June, Seán MacBride outlined how his relationship with Noël Browne had come apart. 'It was some time in the early part of 1950 that I began to notice a change in Dr Browne's attitude. He tended to develop a dictatorial and domineering attitude and sought to create dissension on various issues, most of which were unimportant . . . finally last November I decided that I should have a frank discussion with Dr Browne and should ensure that he understood fully the damage that would results from any internal dissension of this nature.' MacBride reported that Browne had denounced Clann, in which he said he no longer had confidence. The Clann leader also added that the Minister for Health said he was not prepared to waste his time in Clann. MacBride quoted Browne as saying that he would have resigned from the government and Clann some time previously were it not for the fact that he 'would regret it afterwards'. In his Árd Fheis speech MacBride also claimed Browne told him he would seek an issue upon which to bring down the government, force a general election and break up the Clann. MacBride later claimed to have told the chairman of the party's National Executive, Donal O'Donoghue, about this meeting with Browne, although Browne himself rejected MacBride's account.

In his reply to MacBride's letter, Noël Browne described the correspondence as 'a model of the two-faced hypocrisy and humbug so characteristic of you'. Browne also took the opportunity to reply to allegations made by MacBride at the Clann party meeting. 'Your references to my immaturity are surely gratuitous. My experience of democratic politics began only a few weeks subsequent to your own. I did not, however, have much to unlearn'. Browne also informed MacBride in that letter that he had informed the party's General Secretary of his resignation from Clann. 'I have bidden farewell to your unwholesome brand of politics.'

In seeking the resignation of his party colleague, MacBride had decided to divide Clann na Poblachta so as to preserve the inter-party government. Throughout the Mother and Child controversy MacBride displayed little of the radicalism which symbolised Clann na Poblachta in its early days. Noël Browne says he was not surprised by MacBride's response. 'I don't think they (Clann members) knew how close MacBride was to the Fine Gael people and to their ideals.' It is true that MacBride had a conservative nature and would have had great difficulty crossing the bishops. As one writer has put it he: 'unquestionably took his religious faith from

Rome - despite his former military activities'. In the late 1930s when Maud Gonne's autobiography was being prepared he is said to have been 'adamant in his insistence that his mother maintain a discreet silence about aspects of her past life'. According to Maud Gonne's biographer, Margaret Ward, these included details of an affair MacBride's mother had with a Frenchman which resulted in the birth of his sister out of wedlock.

The circumstances surrounding the departure of Browne from cabinet led to open division in Clann. His resignation was followed by others. Deputy Jack McQuillan sent a resignation letter dated 12 April to the General Secretary of the party. In it he stated that 'recent happenings with the party have convinced me that the Clann leadership have betrayed the trust placed in them by those who elected them'. He said the controversy over Noël Browne had served only to bring matters to a head. The Roscommon deputy noted: 'The party executive on several occasions has affirmed its support for Dr Noël Browne in the introduction of a non-means test Mother and Child scheme.'

The resignation letter continued: 'While I, of course, accept without question, as a Catholic, the hierarchy's ruling on this scheme, I think it a matter of deep regret that Mr MacBride has not in the last six months informed the executive that the Taoiseach and he had definite knowledge that Dr Browne's scheme would not meet with the approval of the hierarchy.' He went on to address MacBride's lack of support for his colleague at cabinet: ' . . . it is very difficult to understand the motives of Mr MacBride in withholding it.'

In his June Árd Fheis speech MacBride told Clann delegates: 'It became obvious that unless he resigned the Taoiseach would be forced to ask for his resignation. I considered that it would be undesirable to allow this to happen. Dr Browne was a member of the government as my nominee on behalf of the Clann; it was clearly my responsibility to ask him to resign when it became clear that nothing further could be done to make him act responsibly'. It would appear that MacBride feared the Taoiseach, a member of another party, might take the initiative and request Browne's resignation. MacBride said in his Árd Fheis speech that 'Dr Browne was still a member of the Clann and I was still responsible for his presence at cabinet . . . as party leader I had to stand over him so long as he remained in the government as my nominee'.

The departure of Browne took on a further twist when he made public the correspondence between himself, Costello, MacBride and the bishops. The repercussions only added to the sense of crisis surrounding the inter-party government and Clann na Poblachta. In reply Clann issued a public statement which sought to show that Seán MacBride had no choice but to seek the resignation of Browne:

> As it sought to represent that the events leading up to Dr Browne's resignation from Clann na Poblachta have their sole origin in the proposed Mother and Child Health Service, it has become necessary to release for publication the following resolution which was adopted unanimously by

the Ard Comhairle at its meeting of March 31st–
April 1st last: That the Ard Comhairle view with
grave concern and disapproval the attitude and
conduct of Dr Browne and is perturbed by his
lack of co-operation and by his apparent disloyalty
to the leadership of the party and require him to
show a greater degree of loyalty and co-operation
in his dealings with the leadership. The Ard
Comhairle reiterates its support for the Mother
and Child Service but it considers it necessary
however to express its fear that the successful
implementation of this service may be jeopardised
by the manner in which the whole problem is
being handled by Dr Browne . . .

Significantly this new statement claimed:

that the Ard Comhairle wish to put on record
that if the leader of the party deems it necessary
to call for the resignation or removal of Dr
Browne from the government, he can rely on
the support of the Ard Comhairle. Dr Browne's
lack of candour, irresponsibility and disloyalty
had been considered by the Coiste Seasmhach
and the Ard Comhairle for some months . . .
and the foregoing resolution was adopted only
after the most careful consideration, in a final
effort to avoid the position which he has now
deliberately created. They were not published

> or circularised to the organisation until all
> hope that Dr Browne would behave responsibly
> had to be abandoned . . .

Browne's resignation as Minister for Health was debated in the Dáil on 12 April. In a short speech he said he accepted the ruling of the bishops but that Clann and the government had already promised the electorate a free health scheme. The *Irish Times* reported that when Browne sat down he received applause from all sides in the House. Nevertheless, the Taoiseach claimed the speech was full of 'inaccuracies, misstatements and misrepresentations'. The debate on Browne's resignation was marked by bitterness among the former Clann deputies and those who still remained loyal to the party. Independent deputy Oliver Flanagan, who was later to join Fine Gael, noted: 'This is a family row within the Clann.' Captain Peadar Cowan said it struck him 'as a thunderbolt . . . to learn that a situation had arisen in which one of the most popular ministers in the government was on the verge of being dismissed or resigning'. This situation had arisen, Cowan claimed, because Browne 'was more popular than his leader . . . '. He also described MacBride ' . . . as one of the most dangerous characters in this country'. Con Lehane interrupted Cowan's contribution to note that 'all that is wrong with the deputy is that his connection with Clann na Poblachta ended very suddenly', to which the former Clann deputy replied 'and very fortunately'.

The inter-party government was weakened by the divisions

in Clann. After just over three years in office its ability to govern had been threatened by the defections of several deputies from its ranks. In addition, the economic situation, while improving, was not getting real benefits through to people quickly enough. Several weeks after the Dáil debate on Browne's resignation, a number of rural deputies threatened to withdraw their support unless the price of milk was raised to help farm incomes. In an environment of threats to the continuation of the inter-party administration as a credible government, John A. Costello decided that it was time to go to the country.

6

ON THE OUTSIDE LOOKING IN

Clann na Poblachta faced into the 1951 general election divided and with massive defections. Of the ten Clann TDs elected in 1948, three stood as Independents and another joined the Labour Party. The war of words continued between the party and its now departed former colleagues. One statement issued by the party claimed 'the events of the recent week have come as a severe shock to the rank and file of Clann na Poblachta and to the public . . . these events are only a step in a determined effort to wreck the Clann . . . ' The North Mayo Comhairle Ceanntair issued a statement in which it 'unanimously' affirmed ' . . . complete and unquestionable belief in Seán MacBride's leadership of Clann na Poblachta and repudiates wholeheartedly Dr Browne's futile attempt at dictatorship'. However, such statements were no substitute for action to help the party to maintain a relevant political presence.

Unlike 1948 there was no ambition to replace Fianna Fáil as the dominant party. In 1948 Clann had nominated candidates in every constituency; on this occasion it fielded only twenty-six candidates in total. Consolidation and survival was now the policy. There were no Clann candidates in any of the five constituencies in Cork, in either of the two Donegal constituencies or in Kildare, Laois-Offaly, Limerick West, Louth, Mayo South, Meath, Monaghan, Waterford and Wicklow. Nor were there any Clann candidates in Dun Laoghaire-Rathdown or Dublin North-East. Clann had won a seat in each of these two constituencies in 1948. Now, in 1951, Peadar Cowan ran as an independent in Dublin North-East while in Dun Laoghaire-Rathdown Joseph Brennan stood for the Labour Party. The two other Clann deputies who ran as independents in 1951 were Noël Browne in Dublin South East and Jack McQuillan in Roscommon.

In 1948 Clann had no difficulty in finding candidates. In many constituencies two or three names were nominated to represent the party. Three years later Clann was unable to find candidates even in constituencies where it had local councillors elected in the 1950 local elections. Clann was able to nominate more than one candidate in only four constituencies. As in 1948 the party had two candidates in the three-seat Kerry South constituency but on this occasion, the party had two new candidates, John O'Leary and Jeremiah O'Riordan. O'Leary had been elected to Kerry County Council for the Killarney Area at the 1948 local elections. It would appear that O'Riordan had little political experience. A butcher and cattle dealer, he made news even before nominations closed. The *Kerryman* newspaper reported how he 'tendered a cheque for his election deposit' but was told that only payment with cash was acceptable. 'There then followed a ten-minute dash to and from a friend in Tralee who cashed the £100 cheque and Mr O'Riordan got in just in time.'

Seán MacBride embarked on a tour of the constituencies where Clann candidates were proposed. He was reported to have addressed a crowd of about two thousand people in Tralee. In Kerry North the party had only one candidate in 1951, although there was the advantage that this candidate, John Connor, had run in the previous general election. He had won a council seat in the previous local elections in Kerry.

Apart from Kerry South, it was only in MacBride's own constituency of Dublin South-West, in Dublin South-Central and in Longford–Westmeath that Clann was able to nominate more than a single candidate. In Carlow-Kilkenny there had been three candidates in the 1948 general election but only Patrick Gleeson ran in 1951. A similar situation existed throughout the country. There had been three Clann candidates in Limerick East in 1948; in 1951 only Ted Russell ran again. In Mayo North Martin McGrath stood again but stood alone; in the previous general election he had been one of three candidates. Seamus O'Neill in Wexford was in the same situation. When John Timoney won a seat in 1948 he was one of three Clann candidates in Tipperary South; three years later he was the sole Clann nomination.

In some constituencies Clann selected candidates who had run in the previous general election. These included Fionán Breathnach in Dublin North-Central, Michael Kelly in Roscommon and in Galway South Vincent Shields, who had been elected to Galway County Council at the 1950 local elections. They had all had party colleagues on the ticket in 1948; this time they stood as the sole Clann candidate in their respective constituency. A similar situation faced three of the party's outgoing TDs: Deputy John Tully in Cavan, Deputy Michael Fitzpatrick in Dublin North-West and Deputy Patrick Kinnane in Tipperary North. All three stayed with Clann to defend their seats although none had a running mate in 1951.

In a number of constituencies Clann's candidates were newcomers. Those who had contested the previous general election had either parted with Clann or stood aside on this occasion. These included candidates in constituencies like Dublin County, Dublin South-East, Galway West, Galway North and Sligo-Leitrim.

The *Sligo Champion* wrote that the general election was a 'turning point', but an analysis of the local newspaper throughout the campaign makes it clear that the Mother and Child controversy did not dominate debate. As the *Sligo Champion* noted there was 'a clear-cut issue before the electors - whether they want an inter-party government or a Fianna Fáil government'. Despite the break-up of the government there was still a great degree of co-operation between the parties which had made up that administration. For them all the enemy was still de Valera and Fianna Fáil. One of the Fine Gael candidates in Sligo-Leitrim requested his supporters to continue their voting preferences 'for the other Fine Gael and inter-party candidates in the order of your choice'. Clann posters in Laois-Offaly asked party voters to continue their preferences to inter-party candidates.

Clann was going to need all the assistance it could get; the events leading up to the collapse of the inter-party government had certainly hurt the party. The resignations of key members, like Browne and Cowan, were big losses. As in previous electoral contests the party lacked an organised structure. This was evident around the country and it was probably as much to blame for the disarray among Clann activists as the divisions over the Mother and Child controversy. Writing in the *Nationalist and Leinster Times*, Barney Boland noted the 'sympathetic good wishes of a great many ordinary Irish people' as regards the Mother and Child scheme. He observed that the affair had been complicated by the side-issue of the split in Clann. Indeed, Councillor Patrick Gleeson from Kilkenny claimed the 'number of defections was negligible' in his constituency.

In several parts of the country, however, the divisions in Clann were clearly evident. The *Roscommon Champion* newspaper reported: 'The Clann na Poblachta party in Roscommon has split over the resignation from the Clann of Deputy Jack McQuillan'. The situation has led, the newspaper said, to 'great activity in Clann circles in the county' and 'hurriedly convened meetings'. These meetings were 'the subject of lengthy, and in some cases, it was learned, heated discussions'. The Clann organisation in Stokestown passed a resolution pledging 'unswerving loyalty to the Clann under the leadership of Mr MacBride'. Jack McQuillan's actions were 'deplored' by Clann members in

Boyle, who were unhappy that he had not consulted his constituents. But a party meeting in Castlerea congratulated McQuillan for resigning 'as a result of the undemocratic action of Mr Seán MacBride' in seeking Noël Browne's resignation as Minister for Health.

Like Browne and Peadar Cowan, Jack McQuillan stood as an independent candidate in the 1951 general election. During the election campaign he rounded on his former party. 'I have often criticised Fianna Fáil on the grounds that they were a one-man party. I have to admit now that a far worse dictatorship exists within the ranks of Clann na Poblachta.' He referred to the party he had left as the 'now dwindling Clann'. In one of his election notices, published in the *Roscommon Champion*, McQuillan declared that his only regret was he 'didn't break with the Clann much earlier'. He also alleged that 'the Clann standing committee looked at Ireland through the eyes of Dublin'.

The party's first General Secretary, Michael Kelly, had run in the 1948 election in Roscommon, polling 2,660 first preference to 3,025 first preferences for McQuillan. In 1951 Kelly became Clann's standard bearer in the constituency. Although he increased his own personal vote marginally to 2,751 votes it was not enough to preserve Clann's seat in Roscommon. McQuillan was elected as an independent with 3,666 first preferences, taking the last of the four seats on offer. Commenting on the outcome, the *Roscommon Herald* noted that 'there was a shattering decline in Clann na Poblachta's fortunes'.

The party's vote slumped around the country. It won only

two seats, in Cavan and Dublin South-West. Cavan, where John Tully held his seat, was the only constituency where the party's vote increased. In 1948, with two candidates, Clann took just over 15 per cent of the vote in the constituency. That percentage rose to just under 19 per cent in 1951, with Tully receiving over 6,400. MacBride held his own seat in Dublin South-West although his vote was down substantially and he only managed to take the final seat in this five-seat constituency. He got only 2,800 first preferences. One of his opponents was a former Clann member who had resigned from the party when Browne left. To Clann's embarrassment Michael Ffrench O'Carroll actually polled nearly 3,000 more first-preferences votes than MacBride.

The other four deputies elected in 1948 who stayed loyal to Clann but lost their seats in 1951 were Con Lehane, John Timoney, Patrick Kinnane and Michael Fitzpatrick. In Dublin North-West, Fitzpatrick's vote totally disappeared. In 1948 he had received almost 2,400 first preferences. That vote was down to nearly 460 first preferences in 1951 which was less than two per cent of the total first-preference vote in the constituency. Despite his impressive Dáil record and activity in Clann, Con Lehane lost out in Dublin South-Central. John Timoney's seat in Tipperary South was always marginal given the narrowness of his victory in 1948. Therefore, his defeat in the circumstances was not unexpected. The loss of Patrick Kinnane's seat in Tipperary North was a greater blow. It was his third electoral contest in four years and Clann's vote was halved in the constituency.

The situation for the four deputies who had resigned

from Clann was a lot better. Jack McQuillan, who was returned as an independent for Roscommon, was joined in the new Dáil by two former Clann deputies, Noël Browne and Peadar Cowan. Browne had been successful as an independent candidate in Dublin South-East, taking nearly 29 per cent of the first-preference vote in that constituency. Peadar Cowan in Dublin North-East also held his seat. Although his first-preference vote was down 1,000 votes to 3,600, Cowan was re-elected as an independent. However, it was not all good news for the former Clann deputies. In Dun Laoghaire-Rathdown Joseph Brennan, who had left Clann for the Labour Party, was defeated.

Support for Clann was always likely to be affected, given all the bad feeling surrounding the last months of the inter-party government and its acrimonious break-up. The party was certain to find its second general election tough going. In many constituencies a skeleton organisation existed, while in places like Cork there was no Clann presence at all. The successes of government, Browne's hospital building programme and MacBride's profile in External Affairs, had not been capitalised upon in a concrete manner.

In addition, it was probably inevitable that traditional Fianna Fáil supporters, who had supported Clann in 1948, would return to de Valera. Many of the republican constituency had felt let down by the new party as early as 1948, when it entered government with the old enemy Fine Gael. So without this republican vote and with much of its radical/welfarist support dissipated on account of the Mother and Child controversy, Clann na Poblachta in 1951 was not the new dawn it had promised to be in 1948.

Although Fianna Fáil increased its first preference vote it gained only one extra seat. The two Labour groupings had merged in 1950. Although Labour increased its vote on the previous election it actually came back in 1951 with three fewer seats. Clann na Talmhan was down one seat to six. Fine Gael were the big winners, taking almost 26 per cent of the first preference vote and an extra nine seats. The 1951 general election returned seventeen independent deputies, their ranks swelled by the three former Clann deputies.

Despite the break-up of Costello's administration, an inter-party formation was still a possibility when the results were known but it would have required the support of too many independent deputies to be a stable formation. Many independents like Noël Browne and former Clann member, now Dáil deputy, Michael Ffrench O'Carroll, would not have voted for a government that included Seán MacBride.

In the Dáil MacBride, now one of two Clann deputies, called for the formation of 'a nationally representative government'. He spoke of 'appeals' made to de Valera in the days prior to the election of a new Taoiseach and government to form such an administration. In any event it was Fianna Fáil that formed the new government. Despite being five seats short of an overall majority de Valera managed to obtain the support of several independents, including former Clann members.

MacBride and Tully played their part in Dáil debates but there was a degree of embarrassment that there were more former Clann deputies in the Dáil than re-elected Clann

TDs. In addition, Noel Hartnett had been elected to the Seanad. Tensions remained, although Peadar Cowan spoke of the need 'to endeavour to avoid being in conflict . . . '

As a former Minister for External Affairs, MacBride made a point of speaking on international issues, although it is fair to say that ending partition was still his main objective. He also contributed to debates on economic matters, reiterating Clann policies in areas like afforestation. On one occasion he asked the Minister for Education if he would 'make available to all national schools suitably framed copies of the Proclamation of 1916 and request that these be displayed in all the classrooms'.

The new Fianna Fáil government dealt efficiently with Browne's health legislation but it was unable to address the serious economic and social problems which the country still faced. The previous government's establishment of the IDA and the Export Board was still too recent to have had any impact in expanding the industrial base. In any event, dominant Fianna Fáil thinking still put most of its faith in the agricultural sector. In its first budget the new government increased income taxation while allowing the price of food and petrol to rise. These were hardly policies to win public support, never mind turning around the economy. Emigration and unemployment continued to be a normal feature of everyday life. The policies of de Valera's government were unpopular and the electorate gave its judgement at a series of nine by-elections, three of which were held in June 1952.

Clann faced into the by-election in Limerick East in a relatively strong position. In Ted Russell it had a candidate who had contested the two previous general elections in that constituency, polling just over 5,000 first preferences in the 1951 general election. Fine Gael, Fianna Fáil and Labour also contested the Limerick East by-election, which had been caused by the death of one of the Fianna Fáil TDs in the constituency. The Clann candidate was expected to challenge for the seat but when the result was declared Clann had increased its vote by only 2.5 per cent. The *Limerick Leader* noted that Clann did 'not appear to have done as well as was generally expected' in the 1952 by-election.

Like Russell, the party's candidate in the Mayo North by-election had contested the two previous general elections. Martin McGrath was also a county councillor. He had polled over 3,100 first preferences in 1951. The Mayo by-election had been caused by the death of P. J. Ruttledge, who had been a member of each Fianna Fáil cabinet from 1932 until he resigned on health grounds in 1942. McGrath increased Clann's vote to nearly 20 per cent but was far from taking the seat. The party did not nominate a candidate for the third June 1952 by-election, which was in Waterford. Despite the election of a councillor in Waterford at the 1950 local elections no progress had ever been made at putting in place a coherent party structure.

The weakness of the party in constituencies like Waterford was evident from a number of these by-elections. There were no Clann candidates nominated for the by-elections in Cork East (June 1953), Cork Borough (March 1954) or Louth (March 1954). None of these constituencies had been contested by Clann since the 1948 general election.

A by-election was held in Wicklow on the same day as Cork East. Again there had been no Clann presence in Wicklow since 1948. However, one of the two candidates at that election, William Clarke, was persuaded to stand at the by-election. The party was unable to pull off a surprise and received less than 10 per cent of the first preference poll.

The electoral defeats at the Cork Borough and Louth by-elections, both held in March 1954, contributed to de Valera's going to the country two months later. In the Dáil at that time, MacBride claimed: 'what the people of the country want is an efficient and competent government. I think they are sick and tired of these internal wrangles about the civil war and about personalities of one kind or another.' He went on to say that he believed the electorate wanted 'a national government with certain fixed objectives, such as the ending of partition, the development of our resources and the saving of the Gaelteacht'.

These were the issues the Clann leader raised at meetings around the country during the 1954 general election campaign. During this campaign electoral broadcasts were permitted for the first time on Radio Éireann. The *Sligo Champion* noted that: 'all the talks heard up to the moment of writing were of the type that civil servants can prepare so expertly. They were ponderous affairs - full of long sentences, stuffed with statistics and replete with every well-worn political cliché.'

Since 1952, efforts had been made to revive Clann as a political force. The party had been presented with nine by-elections to upset the political establishment, as it had done in October 1947 when MacBride and Kinnane were elected. Yet it failed to register a single win and in 1954 only twenty candidates were nominated. That was six fewer than in the previous general election. Talk of electing a single party Clann government was now only a memory from the distant days of 1948, when great expectations were invested in the new political party.

There were familiar names among those who stood for Clann in 1954. These included Fionán Breathnach in Dublin North Central, Joseph Barron in Dublin South Central, Vincent Shields in Galway South, John O'Leary in Kerry South, Martin McGrath in Mayo North and Martin McGowan in Sligo-Leitrim. For most of these candidates it was to be their final attempt at seeking election to Dáil Éireann. Patrick Kinnane stood in Tipperary North in an attempt to win back the seat he had held from the end of 1947 until his defeat in the 1951 general election. The candidates were joined by outgoing Cavan deputy John Tully and, of course, Clann's leader Seán MacBride.

There were also newcomers among the candidates nominated by Clann. Two new candidates stood in the Roscommon constituency in the 1954 general election. They were John Scott, a farmer and solicitor, who had unsuccessfully contested the 1950 local elections for Clann, and another local solicitor, Michael Garvey. MacBride visited the constituency on his leader's tour. The meeting had a 'fairly good attendance of people who listened attentively to the speakers'. Among the issues MacBride spoke on was depopulation due to emigration. An advertisement for the party in the *Roscommon Champion* said that 'Unlike the old-established political parties, Clann na Poblachta has not collected vast funds; and to contest its third general election in the short space of six years, your help is urgently needed'.

An advertisement for the party in the *Clare Champion* asked people to 'join on the road that leads to progress and prosperity with Clann na Poblachta'. It outlined the party's manifesto, which included policies such as guaranteed agricultural prices, increased food subsidies to assist the housewife and a promise of reducing taxation by ending extravagance. There were also old Clann policies such as 'a vigorous policy of afforestation', the re-integration of the national territory and fostering the national language and culture.

Having been beaten in the 1952 by-election in Limerick East, Ted Russell stood aside on this occasion. Steve Coughlan was Clann's candidate in 1954. He ran under the slogan, 'The Housewives' Choice'. Coughlan was one of the unlucky stories of the 1954 general election. He lost out by only ninety-four votes on the seventh and final count to the Labour Party deputy M. J. Keyes. Transfers played a crucial role in the constituency. However, they did not go Clann's way as Coughlan had been six hundred first preference votes ahead of Keyes on the first count. In defeat Coughlan said of Clann: 'We are still young and we will come again.'

There were similar fighting words from the Clann candidate in Clare, Seán O'Connor, an assurance represent-ative from Miltown Malbay. He had joined the party at its inception, was a member of the national executive and had been elected to Clare County Council at the 1950 local elections. The party's director of elections was Tim Smythe. He had contested the 1948 general election and was also a member of Clare County Council. Despite everyone's best efforts the result was no better than in 1948 when Clann had previously contested the Clare constituency. When the results were known O'Connor said he entered the election in the knowledge that he would not be elected. However, he said he would run again as Clann 'had something to offer to the people, something which they may not be prepared to follow for the moment but would later on when they got educated on what Clann had put before them'.

In Kerry North John Connor stood for the third time for Clann. He declared that the party was committed to a policy of restoration of subsidies for essential foodstuffs. Seán MacBride spoke at a meeting in Tralee. In his address he touched on the now familiar Clann issue of an All-Ireland parliament and declared that there could be no freedom for Irish citizens without economic freedom.

Connor had been beaten in 1948 and 1951, although in keeping Clann's vote at 12.6 per cent in the latter election he had done well in difficult circumstances. His election literature described him as 'a practical farmer who earns his livelihood solely from farming'. A local councillor, Connor had chaired Kerry County Council so he was well known in the constituency. Interestingly, he asked Clann supporters in their lower preference votes to 'support inter-party candidates'. This may be a pointer that even with only twenty candidates nominated Clann was still considering the option of a return to an inter-party arrangement after the election.

Clann's first-preference vote in the Kerry North constituency was up some 550 votes. With the help of transfers this was enough to give the Clann candidate the last seat. Connor's victory meant that Clann came out of the 1954 election with an additional Dáil deputy. This was despite a decrease of 3,000 in its total first-preference vote; with just over 51,000 votes Clann took only 3.8 per cent of the total national vote. This was enough to elect MacBride, Tully and their new colleague John Connor.

The Fine Gael revival, which began in 1951, continued for the party in this general election. Of all the parties which had participated in the first inter-party government Fine Gael benefited most. After a decade of decline, power gave credibility back to Fine Gael. In 1944 Fianna Fáil had seventy-six seats with Fine Gael holding thirty. The outcome of the 1954 general election gave Fianna Fáil sixty-five seats with Fine Gael, on the back of a revival in its fortunes, returning fifty deputies. The Fine Gael candidate in Kerry South declared after his election that the surplus of inter-party votes over those for Fianna Fáil in the constituency represented a defeat for Fianna Fáil. This led to uproar in the count centre. Gardai had to intervene and the new Fine Gael deputy had to leave the stage where speeches were being made without finishing his words of thanks. But this was the reality of the election outcome. The additional ten seats for Fine Gael put the party in a strong position to lead a second inter-party administration.

Speaking in the Dáil on the nomination of the new Taoiseach, the Clann leader reiterated his now familiar belief in the value of national government. 'I believe that the best type of government which would serve the interests of the nation in the present situation is a government that would be representative of all the principal parties in this House.' So convinced was MacBride of the merits of this form of government that he submitted proposals to the other party leaders. Clann envisaged a national government as setting out to achieve four objectives. These were the reunification of the county, full employment, saving the Gaelteacht and providing efficient administration. Clann reasoned that a united effort was necessary to achieved these objectives. Such a formation was never a realistic proposal and Clann had to deal with the numbers game as thrown up by the outcome of the 1954 general election.

The nomination of Costello and that of his new government thus won the backing of the three Clann deputies. Soon after the results became known, Costello had won agreement for an administration involving Fine Gael, Labour and Clann na Talmhan. This formation had a total of seventy-four seats out of a total of 147 on offer. Costello needed Clann to be certain of a majority.

In the days prior to the meeting of the Dáil the newspapers reported that Clann would accept an invitation to join the new administration. It was believed that if Clann agreed to enter government its leader would be given his old External Affairs portfolio. On the topic of which grouping to support for the formation of a government, MacBride observed: 'In so far as the issue of the recent election was between the concept of a one-party and the concept of a representative inter-party government, the people have expressed their wish in unmistakable terms. They have clearly opted for an inter-party government'. However, Clann only offered external support for the second-inter party government. It was believed that the party's TDs wanted to enter government but that Clann's national executive overruled them. MacBride announced the decision 'with regret'. He admitted there was no difference of policy or any dissatisfaction with the department offered. Explaining the decision, MacBride reasoned that with only three deputies Clann was not entitled to representation in government and that 'the acceptance of a post would be invidious'. He added his reservation that ultimately he would find himself ' . . . in the position of a lodger who was not paying for his keep'. Whatever about the excuses offered by MacBride, there was also the rejection by his party's executive of a re-run of the experience of government of 1948-51. Many believed that Clann could be better rebuilt in opposition and without dealings with Fine Gael.

Despite being outside government, Clann received some of the spoils of office in return for its 'external support'. In 1954, with MacBride's support, Liam Kelly from County Tyrone was elected to the Seanad on the Oireachtas sub-panel of the Labour panel. Kelly had established a fringe republican group, Fianna Uladh, after being expelled by the IRA for unauthorised military activity. His group recognised the legitimacy of Dáil Éireann. The Clann leader hoped that Kelly would be followed by others in the IRA who would reject absentionism. Kelly in fact made little use of his new position and like the two previous members of that Chamber associated with Clann he did little for the party. In fact it was the end of 1955 before Kelly made his first contribution in the Seanad. That speech on the development and preservation of Gaelteacht areas was also his last, although it was not the last that was heard of Kelly himself.

Clann went into the 1955 local elections seeking support to establish 'clean, efficient and impartial administration'. It had candidates running in twenty-one of the thirty-one councils, five fewer council areas than it had contested at the previous local elections. Many of the constituencies where it ran candidates were those in which it had secured their election in 1950: areas like Clare, Limerick Corporation and Roscommon. In Limerick both Steve Coughlan and Ted Russell consolidated Clann's presence on the City Council. The two men were re-elected on the first count, well exceeding the quota of 1,015 votes. Coughlan was ahead on this occasion with 1,930 votes, while Russell received 1,420 votes. Russell had gone into election holding the city mayoralty. These votes meant that two of the four aldermen positions in Limerick City Council were held by Clann councillors.

John Danager had unsuccessfully contested the 1950 local elections for Clann. Five years later, in 1955, he was elected and joined Coughlan and Russell on the city council. Out of six candidates Clann had three elected. But any sense of celebration soon disappeared as rivalry between Russell and Coughlan surfaced. The first public display of disquiet in Clann circles in Limerick City was over an arrangement to rotate the mayoralty between different groupings on the council. Russell, who had so narrowly missed out on the position in 1950, was in favour of such an arrangement, while others in the party were opposed. Russell had unanimous support for re-election but withdrew his name and shortly afterwards left Clann altogether.

In Roscommon Peter McGuinness was elected in the Elphin area, while the party also took a seat in Boyle. In 1950 Clann won two seats in the Roscommon area but after the controversy of 1951 these two councillors (one of whom was Jack McQuillan) left the party. Clann had opted out of the general election contest in Carlow-Kilkenny in 1954 even though one of its members was Mayor of Kilkenny at the time. Patrick Gleeson had stood for Clann in the 1948 and 1951 general elections. He was re-elected to Kilkenny County Council in 1955. In Clare Seán O'Connor and Tim Smythe were re-elected. Both headed the poll in their respective electoral areas. However, Thomas Lillis, who had by this stage left Clann, held the seat he won for the party in 1950 but this time as an independent candidate.

In total, Clann won twenty-one council seats on twelve county councils, a loss of only five seats on the previous elections. Given the turmoil the party had gone through since 1950, and the defections of several leading members who had been elected at the previous local contest, the outcome was positive. It must be remembered, however, that

Clann was starting from a low base, given its relatively poor performance in 1950. Clann gained seats in Cavan, North Tipperary and Wicklow, with two new seats in Carlow. On the down side the party lost its two councillors on Dublin and Monaghan councils as well as one seat in Donegal, Kerry, Mayo, South Tipperary, Roscommon and Westmeath. However, Clann secured representation for the first time on Galway and Wexford Borough Councils.

In total Fianna Fáil won an additional two council seats, taking its total to three hundred and one. The results were good news for the three parties in the inter-party government. Combined with Clann, which was offering the government external support, these parties took sixteen extra seats.

The inter-party government needed all the help it could get as the economic situation in the country had really not improved since the ending of the Second World War. The government had sought to address balance of payment problems with restrictions on exports of certain goods. One result was even more unemployment. Emigration increased to an annual rate of 80,000 people. People took to the streets. Some of these protest marches resulted in clashes with the gardai. The death of the Fine Gael TD for Limerick West gave Fianna Fáil an opportunity. Clann did not nominate a candidate for the by-election, which was held in December 1955. Michael Colbert of Fianna Fáil came out of retirement to stand for the party. He was elected with 56 per cent of the first preference vote.

At another by-election two months later the government parties played a shrewd game. John Connor died in a motoring accident in December 1955 as he was returning from Dublin to his home in Tralee. The fifty-four-year old Clann deputy had attended a meeting of the party's national executive the previous day and his car was involved in an accident on the main Tralee–Castleisland–Abbeyfeale road. Local paper said the roads were 'slippy from rain'. Many well known Clann figures attended his funeral, including Dr McCartan, Tom Roycroft and Con Lehane. Seán MacBride gave the graveside oration.

The late deputy's daughter was selected to contest the by-election. Kathleen O'Connor was a twenty-two-year old national school teacher who had trained at Carysfort in Dublin. While in Dublin she used to do her father's secretarial work in the Dáil. Up to a short time before her father's death she had been living in Dublin and had only just returned to a teaching post at Meen National School in Knocknagoshel. In a rare case of political solidarity Fine Gael decided to support Kathleen O'Connor. The logic behind their decision, however, probably had more to do with the desire to ensure a Clann seat was not lost to Fianna Fáil. The Minister for Education, Richard Mulcahy, said the Clann candidate made 'an outstanding contribution to the strength of that spirit of co-operation which marked the working of the parties forming the inter-party government'.

MacBride led the campaign in the constituency, although government ministers spoke at Clann meetings in favour of Kathleen O'Connor. Seán MacEoin and Brendan Corish were named in Clann advertisements in local newspapers as addressing party meetings. Three sitting TDs in Kerry, including Dan Spring of Labour, placed an advertisement in the *Kerryman* appealing to their supporters to vote for the Clann candidate. Seán Lemass of Fianna Fáil accused Fine Gael and the other government parties of playing 'the sympathy card'. Fianna Fáil selected Daniel J. Moloney, a garage owner from Listowel, as their candidate. He was a member of Kerry County Council and the Fianna Fáil national executive.

The Taoiseach, John A. Costello, added to the government backing for a candidate from a party which was offering it only external support. He spoke at a Clann rally and put his signature to an advertisement in the *Kerryman* which was headed 'A message from the Taoiseach' and addressed to 'the electors of North Kerry'. In the text of that message Costello told the electorate that it had to choose between two candidates. One of these was 'committed in advance to his party's policy of obstructing the government, the other, O'Connor, will work for the people of North Kerry thorough co-operation with the government'. He added that it was 'therefore, in your interest, and in the interest of the nation at large that you vote Number 1 in this by-election for Miss Kathleen O'Connor.' Costello said her election 'would send a message of encouragement to the government'.

Kathleen O'Connor told one meeting that 'as a youngster in Dingle, and in other parts of Kerry, I came to appreciate the urgent necessity of securing industries, of establishing forestry, and developing the fishing industry to provide employment and increased earnings'. The young national school teacher added that having been 'brought up on a

Kerry farm, I learned the vital importance of securing good and stable prices for livestock, milk and other farm produce'.

O'Connor's vote was nearly four times as large as that received by her father at the previous general election, although, despite all the help from the government parties, her vote was nearly three thousand votes less than the combined votes received by Clann, Fine Gael, Labour and Clann na Talmhan. Fianna Fáil added nearly one thousand votes to its 1954 total but it was still not enough to secure the seat. O'Connor was described as the first single woman to be returned to Dáil Éireann since Independence and became the youngest TD ever to be elected to the Dáil.

At the end of 1956 the IRA undertook two raids on RUC barracks. At Roslea barracks in County Fermanagh one of the men involved was killed. Embarrassingly for MacBride and Clann this raid was organised by Liam Kelly, the County Tyrone man they had nominated to the Seanad. Two IRA members were killed in the raid on the other barracks in County Fermanagh. The inter-party government responded by cracking down on the republican movement and Clann's republican constituency could not endorse the government's actions. They dominated the party's national executive and requested the three Clann TDs to withdraw support for the government. MacBride spoke of how easy it would be to bring down the government but added that it would be hard to find an acceptable replacement. This would appear to suggest that the Clann leader was ambivalent about removing Costello's administration from power.

A motion of no confidence in the government was tabled

by Clann, based on the poor economic situation and the Government's actions against the IRA. By withdrawing its support, Clann precipitated the government's fall. Meetings were held between government ministers and MacBride in an attempt to resolve the situation. Although a great deal of pressure was applied to MacBride to reconsider Clann's position he was bound by the decision of his party members. When Fianna Fáil tabled their own no-confidence motion at the end of January the government was placed in an even tighter corner. With the loss of crucial Dáil support, the Taoiseach John A. Costello called a general election. The party whose candidate had received such strong government support in the Kerry by-election had in the end broken that government. Costello spoke for his colleagues when he referred to the 'general disappointment and anger at the sudden decision of Mr MacBride to break with the government at such short notice'.

7

MOVING SLOWLY
TOWARDS THE END

After just under three years in office the second inter-party government faced the electorate. It had little to offer the people, having lost much of the innovation and freshness of its earlier period in office. There had been seven by-elections during the lifetime of the second inter-party government but Costello's administration failed to win any of them. Seventy-five year old Éamon de Valera led his party into the election in early March 1957 intent on demolishing the idea that a coalition government could work successfully. The need for a strong united government led by a single party was Fianna Fáil's election theme. There was a dispute at the start of the campaign as to whether Clann should be allocated election broadcast time on Radio Éireann. In the end the party received a single broadcast.

Despite its solid performance in the 1955 local elections, Clann went into the general election of 1957 in a sorry state. The party nominated only eleven candidates. It contested all but one of the eight Dublin constituencies. In some of these it would have been better off not contesting, for example

Dublin South-East, where it had not had a candidate since 1951. The party's candidate there polled fewer than four hundred votes. The only non-Dublin constituencies contested were Limerick East, Cavan, Mayo South and Tipperary North.

In Limerick East Steve Coughlan adopted his now common individual slogan to underpin his campaign. This time he appealed to the electorate in Limerick East to 'Stay with Coughlan . . . The righteous are bold.' His vote, however, was down on the 1954 general election by just over 1,000 votes. Coughlan also had to watch as one of the four seats in the constituency was taken by the former Clann member Ted Russell. He stood as an independent candidate having been a Clann nominee at the 1948 and 1951 general elections as well as the 1952 by-election. In 1957 Russell polled almost 2,000 more first preferences than Coughlan.

Although Clann had been successful in the by-election in North Kerry the previous year, the party did not contest the general election in that constituency. By not nominating a candidate, Clann abandoned the North Kerry seat which had first been won at the third attempt by the late John Connor and held by his daughter in the 1956 by-election. She declined to go forward. At a selection convention held in Tralee, Seán MacBride explained that when she agreed to stand at the by-election it was on the clear understanding she would not be expected to stand at the following general election. There had been no previous mention of this 'understanding'. However, if it did exist the party may be accused of poor planning in not identifying an alternative standard-bearer for the general election.

No name emerged from the convention. A Caoimghin Ó Cinneide was later selected to replace O'Connor for Clann but he subsequently withdrew and the party was left without any presence. At the Kerry North convention MacBride declared that Clann hoped 'after this election to be in a position to force the adoption of a comprehensive long-term economic programme and to secure its implementation by a national government.' But without candidates this was going to be a problem. Winning new seats was a big challenge for Clann. Not nominating candidates to contest constituencies where the party had sitting TDs certainly added to the difficulty of this.

As in previous general elections Seán MacBride played an active role in the campaign. Clann held opening and closing rallies at College Green in Dublin. MacBride took the opportunity at the opening rally to reject suggestions that in causing the election, the party was hoping to cash in on the republican sympathy prevailing in the country. He made reference to the 'inertia of government and its policies' as more than ample reason for withdrawing support.

Despite attempts to invigorate Clann's campaign the reality was that the party was on its knees. The failure of so many established Clann councillors to seek election, in constituencies like Carlow-Kilkenny and Clare, was a massive vote of no confidence in the party's ability to do well. In effect the 1957 general election was the beginning of a long-drawn-out end for Clann. It won a mere 20,000 votes and lost seats including that of its party leader, Seán MacBride.

However, in Cavan John Tully held his seat. He maintained his successful record as the only TD elected for Clann in 1948 who had been returned at each subsequent general election. MacBride had had a similar record until this time he lost his seat in Dublin South-West. He had polled only 2,677 first preference votes, a figure down almost 3,500 on his performance in 1954 and even lower than the vote he received in the 1951 general election when controversy surrounded Clann after the divisions within its ranks.

Independent candidate James Carroll increased his vote on the previous general election to almost 3,900 votes. He was elected on the tenth count. At that stage there were two candidates left fighting for the last of the five seats in Dublin South-West. They were the leader of Clann na Poblachta and Bernard Butler of Fianna Fáil. Butler had held a seat in the constituency since 1944. Going into the eleventh count, MacBride was five hundred and seventy-one votes ahead of Butler. However, of Carroll's transferable vote a massive 87 per cent went to the Fianna Fáil candidate. These transfers put Butler on a total of 6,008 votes to Seán MacBride's 5,390 and gave the last seat in Dublin South-West to Fianna Fáil.

Overall, Fianna Fáil won seventy-eight seats in the 1957 general election. This was enough to give de Valera's party its first overall majority in over a decade. Four Sinn Féin candidates won Dáil seats although the party did not take their seats. Clann was reduced to a sole member, John Tully in Dáil Éireann. The future looked bleak for the party, although those still loyal to it refused to admit as much.

Soon afterwards Clann published a new bulletin which sought to deal with its poor electoral performance and also to get its message across. Entitled *Our Nation*, it first appeared in the summer of 1957 at a cost of three pence. It was later claimed the first issue completely sold out. The editorial stated that 'the situation which faces the country could not be graver. It is our economic survival which is now at stake.' Its objective was to 'serve the purpose of awakening public opinion to . . . the bankruptcy of the policies of the major parties'.

It noted that the election results 'must have been disheartening to Clann', which alone 'appealed on the basis of a positive constructive policy'. The publication offered lame excuses for Clann's electoral predicament. It claimed that 'Clann was not prepared to sacrifice its integrity on grounds of doubtful political expediency. This may have cost Clann seats and votes; in such a situation the task of a minority is an ungrateful one'. Just over a decade after the party's formation there was recognition that the initial objective of supplanting Fianna Fáil was now never going to be achieved.

Subsequent issues of *Our Nation* reiterated some of Clann's main hobby horses, especially with regard to monetary policy. On the subject of emigration the Clann journal claimed: 'It is simply due to our inability and failure to exploit our resources and to organise our economy properly.' A new attitude to tourism was evident in the second issue, dated Autumn 1957, which contained an article on the elimination of coarse fish on the Shannon. The Winter

1957-58 issue of *Our Nation* observed that 'following the highly successful Árd Fheis last year in Limerick City, the Ard-Chomhairle have decided to continue holding the Árd Fheis at provisional centres'. That issue of *Our Nation* contained a number of ads for public houses, bed and breakfasts and restaurants in Galway, the venue for that year's Árd Fheis.

Although by now beginning to be involved in other matters Seán MacBride had not given up on returning to the Dáil. His first attempt was in June 1958, at a by-election in Dublin South-Central. Jack Murphy had been elected in the constituency at the 1957 general election as an Independent Unemployed Worker. He had strong republican associations and had gone on hunger strike after his election in protest at the decision to end food subsidies. Disillusioned with political life and under pressure after having been attacked by the Archbishop of Dublin as a communist, he resigned his Dáil seat and went to work in England. In June 1958 a by-election was held to fill this vacancy.

Joseph Barron had run for Clann in Dublin South-Central at each general election since 1948, each time without success. At the selection convention, Barron urged that the candidate selected should be capable of initiating constructive proposal for a planned economy. He endorsed his party's leader as the candidate. *The Irish Times* described MacBride as a 'surprising choice', although as well as Barron's presence in the constituency, Clann also had the knowledge that Con Lehane had taken a seat for the party in Dublin South Central in 1948.

Both Fianna Fáil and Fine Gael nominated candidates. The future Labour Party leader, Frank Cluskey, was the Labour candidate. However, from MacBride's perspective, matters were complicated by the decision of the National Progressive Democratic Party (NPD) to contest the by-election. This party had been formed the previous month by two former Clann deputies, Noël Browne and Jack McQuillan. It had a left-wing policy programme and the ability to hurt MacBride's electoral chances. The choice of Noel Hartnett as the NPD candidate made the by-election even more intriguing for Clann watchers. The two colleagues at the formation and initial successful stage of Clann na Poblachta were now going head-to-head.

The newspapers wrote of 'evidence of a possible recovery by Clann na Poblachta'. MacBride spoke on topics such as unemployment, emigration and the necessity of a planned economy. On the eve of poll most commentators said the outcome would be 'difficult to call'. Torrential rain on voting day was to make the outcome even harder to determine, as only a third of those eligible to vote came out to show their preference.

In the end Fianna Fáil took 34 per cent of the first preferences. However, there was no clear challenger from amongst the other four candidates. Two of them had 17 per cent of the vote while the other two each shared 15 per cent. MacBride was only 905 votes behind Patrick Cummins of Fianna Fáil who was elected on the final count without reaching the quota. As in the previous general election, transfers were to prove the problem for MacBride. Noel

Hartnett's transfers were very anti-Clann. MacBride received only 769 of Hartnett's 2,688 votes, enough to prove costly at the end. But it was his inability to be nearer the Fianna Fáil candidate on the first count which proved the crucial blow. Afterwards, MacBride played down the significance of the defeat saying: 'we are quite pleased with the results, from the party point of view'. The newspapers viewed the Clann defeat in a positive light, writing of the ' . . . re-emergence of Seán MacBride', although, tellingly, not of the re-emergence of Clann na Poblachta.

Twelve months later a by-election was held in Dublin South-West, MacBride's old constituency, caused by the death of Bernard Butler of Fianna Fáil. He had taken the final seat in the constituency at Seán MacBride's expense at the previous general election. Fianna Fáil held three of the seats, Fine Gael had one TD in the constituency and there was an Independent deputy. There were five candidates nominated to contest the by-election, including the Clann leader.

On the first count Joseph Dowling of Fianna Fáil topped the poll with over 9,000 first preferences. MacBride was beaten into third place by Richie Ryan of Fine Gael, who was nearly 1,400 votes ahead of MacBride. However, with the Labour and Sinn Féin candidates having combined votes of nearly 4,000 first preferences there was still a slender hope that MacBride would overtake Ryan. In such an event he would have hoped for a larger share of Ryan's transfers, thus overtaking the Fianna Fáil candidate to take the seat. It was not to be: Richie Ryan took the seat on the fourth count by fifty-six votes.

In the early 1960s, attempts began at realignment of loyalties and ideologies between a number of the opposition parties. There was speculation that Clann would merge with either Clann na Talmhan or the Labour Party. The fact that its leader was not a Dáil deputy, allied with its performance in the 1960 local elections, gave credence to the speculation. Clann needed something to lift it out of the doldrums; otherwise it faced becoming irrelevant. In the 1960 local elections Clann contested very few constituencies. Its slogan was 'On Our Record Alone'. By now it is fair to say Clann nominees had been reduced to seeking personality votes rather than endorsement for the party they represented. Many of those who stood for the party were longstanding standard-bearers.

In Clare the party kept its two seats with long-time members Tim Smythe and Seán O'Connor both being re-elected. However, there was a less favourable outcome for Patrick Gleeson in Kilkenny. He lost his seat on Kilkenny County Council which he had first won ten years earlier. Clann nominated four candidates in Limerick City. With the departure of Ted Russell Clann was left to defend the council seat held by Steve Coughlan and John Danager. Both were re-elected. A well known local soccer player in the League of Ireland, Mick Lipper, also took a seat. By returning three councillors Clann became the second largest party on Limerick Corporation.

The party maintained its presence on Roscommon County Council with the election of Peter McGuinness, a farmer from Tarmonbarry. John Scott, who had first run ten years previously at local level, for the Dáil in 1954 and again at the 1955 council elections, was once more an unsuccessful candidate for Clann. In the Boyle area the party's successful candidate in 1955 topped the poll but he was running this time as an independent having earlier split with Clann.

At the Clann Árd Fheis held in Galway that same year, Seán MacBride argued for the construction of a third force in Irish politics. He spoke in favour of a Republican-Labour Party. This movement was to be 'broadly based', by which he implied support for the merger of Clann, Sinn Féin and the Labour Party. MacBride was of the view that as Labour alone could not win sufficient support to be in government without Fine Gael and Fianna Fáil, it was therefore essential that Labour received the endorsement of the nationalist and republican constituency. The Clann leader claimed that such a grouping ' . . . would ultimately provide an alternative government . . . '

In July, MacBride raised the same issue when addressing a group of university graduates in Moran's Hotel in Dublin. He painted a particularly gloomy picture of the economy, pointing to the high levels of unemployment and emigration. To address these difficulties he called for a rally of the progressive and nationalist forces in the community to provide a dynamic alternative national policy for the people. Although the Clann leader did not elaborate in any great detail on such a policy he did mention the need for state control of banking and the establishment of a state bank to finance a programme of economic expansion.

Brendan Corish, a deputy from Wexford, became leader of the Labour Party in 1960, succeeding William Norton, who had led the party since 1932. Corish had served in both inter-party governments. He was Parliamentary Secretary to the Minister for Local Government and to the Minister for Defence in the first inter-party government in which Clann had participated. Corish was appointed to cabinet in the second inter-party government, holding the post of Minister for Social Welfare.

The new Labour leader was favourably disposed to some form of link with Clann. A document which urged the 'unity of progressive forces' was debated at Labour's 1960 annual conference. Many conference delegates expressed concern about the implications of MacBride and his supporters entering the party. This was especially so given the potential for friction should Noël Browne's NPD also be included in any new alliance. There were worries that the baggage from the break-up of the first inter-party government would lead to hostility between MacBride and Browne. One delegate warned of the danger of 'prostituting our identity'. Another noted that there had been much talk of a third force but what was really needed was a second force. After some four hours of debate the proposal was accepted by the 140 voting delegates, although by a margin of only eighteen votes.

There was a positive response from Clann to the Labour document. A statement was issued which indicated the party's support for Labour's stance and a willingness to co-operate with Labour was expressed. That statement also stressed Clann's policy priorities including the need for 'comprehensive economic planning'. In particular, MacBride wanted greater public direction of credit policy, more control of the state of banks and more scholarships for secondary schools and universities.

At the end of 1960 and into early the following year there were discussions between Clann and Labour about developing a possible alliance. Newspaper reports from the time were generally positive about prospects from the talks. However, fundamental difficulties persisted about the nature and form which any alliance would take. In the first instance, as the trade union movement had about 200,000 members in Northern Ireland, there were bound to be difficulties with Clann's suggestion for the inclusion of nationalist supporters in any alliance. The inclusion of Sinn Féin in the alliance, as suggested by MacBride, would have obvious difficulties for the Labour Party.

Clann members stressed repeatedly that Labour alone could not win sufficient support to govern without Fine Gael and Fianna Fáil. It was therefore essential that the party received the endorsement of the nationalist and republican constituency. However, in Labour Party circles there was a general view that the addition of republicans to the ranks of any new alliance would only confuse matters. It was generally felt that republicans should be joining any new alliance because of their Labour views rather than republican views. The composition of the alliance was a fundamental stumbling block which was never really resolved. Along with the question-mark over Sinn Féin participation, uncertainty persisted about the inclusion of Browne's NPD.

Clann also believed the alliance should be in the form of a merger between the two principal parties involved. The new merger party would have been called 'Labour-Clann' with Brendan Corish as its leader and MacBride taking the deputy leadership. However, there was a less than enthusiastic response from Labour Party people to such a suggestion. They saw Clann as a party which could not even get its leader elected to Dáil Éireann, with little future except as a minor fringe grouping. Conversely they saw the Labour Party as being rejuvenated under its new leader. Labour had twelve Dáil seats, Clann only one. These facts alone led Labour to consider that Clann should dissolve itself and then join Labour. However, an *Irish Times* editorial in December 1960 noted that although Clann had only a single representative in Dáil Éireann, the party 'thanks largely to the quality of its leader commands quite a lot of support throughout the country'.

At the same time that the talks were taking place with Labour there were tentative discussions with Clann na Talmhan and a number of independents about forming a new western-based political party. Representatives from the interested groups met on a number of occasions. County councillors from Cavan, Westmeath, Longford and Roscommon were involved in discussions which do not appear to have gone into any great depth. In an article on the possibilities for a new third force involving Clann the *Hibernian* journal noted that 'The Labour Party's best is not very good, while Clann na Talmhan has no policy at all and the followers of Sinn Féin act without any thought.'

The prospects for any new alliance were not assisted by the deteriorating condition of what was left of the Clann organisation. Seán MacBride's non-membership of Dáil Éireann weakened Clann's request to be treated on a par with Labour in any merger. On the eve of the 1961 general election the Clann cause was not helped by the decision of Steve Coughlan to join the local Labour party and in the process take most of the Limerick Clann organisation with him. The situation in Limerick East typified the situation for Clann. Although the party had come so close on a number of occasions to winning a seat in the constituency there was no Clann candidate in Limerick East at the 1961 general election. Two former members were standing: Ted Russell as an outgoing Independent deputy and Steve Coughlan for Labour.

Joseph Ridge, who ran in the 1950 local elections for Clann, contested the Galway West constituency. In Roscommon another candidate from the 1950 local elections, Peter McGuinness, allowed his name to go forward. His election advertisements in the local newspapers made no mention that he was a Clann na Poblachta candidate. He declared himself to represent issues such as free secondary education, increased number of university scholarships, weekly old aged pensions of three pounds and decentralisation. He also mentioned the by now familiar Clann hobbyhorses of economic planning and opening the Dáil to the elected representatives of the Six Counties. However, neither McGuinness nor Ridge in Galway were successful in their attempts to revive the Clann presence in their respective constituencies.

Clann nominated only five candidates in 1961. Three of these had been candidates in the party's first electoral outing in 1948. Joseph Barron had been one of three Clann candidates in 1948 when Con Lehane took a seat in the constituency for the party. Barron had stayed with Clann but had never come near winning a Dáil seat. The constituency also had the memories of MacBride's near miss at returning to the Dáil at the 1958 by-election when Barron stood aside for his party leader. Despite all the gloom surrounding Clann, Barron again allowed his name to go forward for Clann in the 1961 general election. He polled just over 3,000 first preferences, enough to see him with the help of transfers take the fourth seat in this five-seat constituency. So on his fifth attempt Joseph Barron took a seat in Dublin South Central.

However, this welcome news for Clann was to be negated when the results from Cavan and Dublin South-West became known. Although John Tully in Cavan increased his vote on the previous general election he lost his Dáil seat. The most recent constituency boundaries review had reduced Cavan by one seat to a three-seater. In 1957 Fianna Fáil had taken two seats with the other seats left to Fine Gael and Tully for Clann. Now the Clann member who had held that seat for the party for thirteen years was the one to lose out.

Seán MacBride was again a loser. He received his lowest ever first-preference poll in the constituency and was never near taking a seat. His failure to win a seat precipitated his withdrawal from Irish politics and the end of any aspirations Clann had of ever again being a serious political party.

Indeed, Michael Gallagher has noted that the loss of MacBride's seat ended 'the Clann's remaining pretensions to being a national party as opposed to a label used by a few local-strong individuals'.

The election outcome meant that Clann had little to offer in any talks with the other parties about possible mergers, just a single TD, a number of locally based councillors and a well-thought of leader who could not get elected to the Dáil. Discussions with Labour lingered on for a number of months although they were not a priority for the Labour leadership and no form of agreement was ever finalised. They were formally ended in March 1962.

One writer noted in 1959 that Clann was 'a live body and in spite of its tiny size shows no sign of going out of existence'. But Clann had been struggling since the 1957 general election. The defeat of MacBride and his subsequent failure to get re-elected at two by-elections really meant the end for the party. Increasingly, Seán MacBride became involved in other organisations, which began to take up his time and energy. He had returned to the Bar and became involved in a series of high profile cases both here and abroad. As a former Minister for External Affairs he had maintained his interest in international events and human rights issues. He became active in several international organisations including Amnesty International, of which he became Chairman in 1961. Two years later he was appointed secretary general of the International Commission of Jurists. This interest in international affairs found its way into Clann policy. At the party's 1960 Árd Fheis there were calls on the government of South Africa to release all those who were interned without trial and to observe the provisions of the UN Declaration of Human Rights.

Although MacBride ran in the 1961 general election, the vote he received illustrated the lack of organisation and continuity in Clann efforts. In effect, after the 1961 general election Seán MacBride's involvement in Clann na Poblachta was nearly non-existent. More and more he was abroad. Party meetings were held but few would attend. At the next general election in 1965, the party nominated only four candidates. John Tully staged a comeback in Cavan. Although he actually polled fewer votes than in the previous general election he took the last seat. He was, however, to be the sole Clann Dáil deputy, a role he had previously filled from 1957 to 1961. The party's outgoing deputy, Joseph Barron, lost his seat in Dublin South Central. The fact that MacBride did not stand illustrates his breaking with the party.

A special Árd Fheis was held in July 1965. Although Clann won a seat in the general election of that year, the party was really little more than a collection of independents. Those still involved accepted that there was little to be achieved by continuing as a party. John Tully in the Dáil was essentially an Independent and they had little hope of moving the party from its present marginal position. This special Árd Fheis decided on 10 July 1965 to dissolve Clann na Poblachta. A number of reasons were subsequently given in a statement for the decision to dissolve the party. The members believed that to 'carry on Clann for sentimental reasons when it had ceased to be an effective political force would have been of doubtful political value'.

In addition they listed the results of the three most recent general elections along with several by-elections, all of which demonstrated that the electorate were not prepared to give Clann 'adequate support'. The remaining party members also considered that as Clann had succeeded, directly and indirectly, in achieving some of its 'more spectacular and immediate objectives' there was no need to continue. A third reason for dissolution involved 'a sense of political responsibility which dictated that to be an effective political party required not only a nation-wide active political organisation, but also constant informed analysis of day-to-day policies and events'. They felt it would have been unrealistic, and perhaps even misleading, on the part of Clann to attempt to fulfil this role when it had not the resources necessary to enable it to do so effectively.

The statement recalled some of the changes which Clann claimed it helped to bring about, including participation in the inter-party government which put an end to divisions based on the Civil War; the repeal of the External Relations Act and the enactment of the Republic of Ireland Act; the campaign to eradicate tuberculosis; the development of a forestry programme: a realisation of the importance of economic planning: the retention of proportional represent-ation; and more active participation in European affairs.

The statement also expressed some views on the political future of the country. It noted the tendency to accept unemployment and emigration as an inevitable national structural defect. It called for greater efforts to inform people about the methods and techniques of government as well as economic development in other small countries.

Clann claimed that a much higher standard of education and training, particularly in the technological fields, would be required to achieve full economic expansion. The party saw the diversification of the country's export markets as vitally important. To achieve this there was need for greater imaginative and informed initiatives than had been shown in the past. This was one of the reasons why membership, full or associate, of the European Common Market was considered so vitally important by Clann.

The statement was in a sense a final wish-list from Clann na Poblachta. It said much about where the members saw Clann as it came to an end. It suggested that there should be much greater use for parliamentary committees in considering future legislation and major policy questions. Other views expressed in the lengthy statement were that the system of political patronage in public appointments should be ended as it was objectionable and damaging. The organisation of the civil service was seen as requiring a complete review. It sugested the possibility of the creation of a parliamentary commissioner or ombudsman charged with the function of examining complaints of maladministration and bureaucratic inefficiency and of reporting directly to parliament, and that there should be a system of public annual review of the operation of state-financed corporations.

The Irish Times noted accurately, but somewhat cruelly, that an explanation that Clann had 'gone out of national politics . . . is, perhaps, redundant'. In an editorial article entitled 'Ave Atque Vale' the newspaper said: 'when a party can only secure one seat at a general election its continuance cannot be said to be an answer to any urgent need'. The article traced through the record of Clann from the 'sensational' by-election triumph in 1947 which elected MacBride (forgetting Kinnane's win in Tipperary) to the achievements of the inter-party government. It observed: 'after that the Clann, if it did not actually disappear, faded into the background and assumed the character of the existing scenery'. So nineteen years after Clann na Poblachta was founded it had been dissolved and was gone from the political stage.

8

EPILOGUE

Those last remaining members of Clann na Poblachta who attended its final Árd Fheis in July 1965 decided to maintain contact with each other through a Clann Society. It was envisaged that on occasion it would 'undertake objective studies of problems affecting the national welfare'. This society would not, however, contest elections. In effect, all that remained of Clann at this stage was a number of local organisations. These tended to revolve around a local individual who had the personality to kept some sort of cohesive unit together. John Tully in Cavan was an example. He had been with Clann since its foundation and was the party's last remaining representative in Dáil Éireann. Up to the 1969 general election Tully continued to represent his constituents in Cavan as an independent. He ran as an independent in 1969 but lost his seat and subsequently retired from politics.

Many of the local councillors who still represented Clann in 1965 either retired or ran again as independents. In the 1967 local elections, in Clare, both Tim Smythe and Seán O'Connor, ran as independent candidates. They were two of the few local representatives who had been with Clann since the start. Smythe headed the poll in the Ennis area and was 316 votes above the quota. Interestingly, O'Connor described himself as an 'independent republican'.

So where did it all go wrong? Michael Gallagher has observed that 'like many other minor parties the Clann peaked early and then died a lingering death'. Of the 93 candidates at the 1948 general election only 19 were ever again to stand for Clann. Another six did seek election but for other political parties while the remainder opted out of national political life. Carty has argued that Clann 'was a classic flash party, bursting onto the national electoral scene and then fading just as quickly'. Such a summary is, however, too simplistic. Clann na Poblachta, because of its involvement in the first inter-party government, left a mark on Irish life far in excess of its size.

The inter-party government spent three years and four months in office. Michael Gallagher has said decisions taken by that administration 'had considerable long-term significance, even though they made little contemporary impact'. It would have been a far duller government and certainly less innovative without the influence of Clann. Clann's involvement in that administration can be credited with dealing with issues such as economic planning, the positive role of state intervention, the development of natural resources and a high standard for public officer holders. After years of weariness and poverty, the inter-party government sought to make life a little better for the general public. It instigated a public housing construction drive. It was radical with a small 'r' in challenging the Department of Finance and using state money to fund the construction of houses. Over 1,000 houses were built in 1947, but just over 12,000 were built in 1951. At the same time efforts were made to improve services like electricity provision, piped water and indoor sanitation.

As well as the better-known successes achieved by Clann's two cabinet ministers, they did well at getting some of their pet projects through government. The inter-party government established a commission on emigration as promised in Clann's election manifesto. In 1949 the government abolished the controversial rating system for teachers which had been the cause of so much discontent in the profession. In addition, as promised by Clann, a Council of Education was set up. It had the objective of advising the government on the function of the national school and on the curriculum which was to be taught at that level.

Clann na Poblachta also challenged the orthodox thinking which pervaded the civil service. Both Browne in Health and MacBride in External Affairs pushed out the boundaries of policy in their respective departments. The traditional and accepted way of doing things was challenged in everything from how the Sweepstakes money was spent in Health to the role of the state in the economy with the Marshall Aid Programme.

Clann's two ministers were among the brightest and most radical individuals that have served in any government before or since. Noël Browne's record in the Health Department stands as testimony to what a minister can do with power if driven by a desire to implement real change to make ordinary people better off. When MacBride left office in 1951 the *Kilkenny People* newspaper wrote that the country 'had lost a Minister for External Affairs without peer' who had 'set a standard of achievement that is not likely to be equalled, and certainly will not be surpassed by his successor'.

But these notable successes were not built upon to consolidate Clann's position after 1948 so that it would gain at the following general election. Seán MacBride admitted to making a number of mistakes in his political career. 'Politically, I think probably, my biggest mistake was naming Dr Browne as Minister for Health in the first inter-party government. I did that because he had no associations with the past, and I felt it was necessary to get somebody new who would have a fresh approach to problems. I was criticised for that within my own party on the basis that he was too inexperienced, and so on, and it probably was a mistake.'

This explanation is far too simplistic. Despite their undoubted talents, neither Browne nor MacBride was a born leader. To borrow a phrase, used to describe Browne, to cover both MacBride and Browne - they were good men to have on your side for a battle but not for a long war. To get Clann on the road and into its first government, both men were essential to establish the party. However, to continue down that road with growth, neither was the appropriate figurehead for the new party. The strong nature and impatience associated with their respective personalities were bound to lead to division. Supporters of both men ultimately divided along the lines of their preference.

Joe Lee has written of Seán MacBride's 'ineptness as a party leader' and inability to 'mould an effective working team around him'. Whatever about the former comment the latter is completely true. Seán MacBride as leader of Clann na Poblachta failed after the party entered government to put in place structures to allow Clann to develop. Key figures in the party were not given positions of responsibility. As Minister of External Affairs, MacBride had heavy foreign travel duties. It was always going to be impossible to juggle all these demands. In the end Clann suffered.

The experience in government discredited Clann and ultimately led to its destruction. The initial decision to enter government with Fine Gael shook the support of its republican constituency. Then the manner by which the party left office on the Noël Browne controversy drove away most of its welfarist support. However, it was always likely that Clann would witness conflict among its diverse membership. As early as 1946 when Clann was founded they wanted different things from the newly formed party. As Noël Browne has written: 'Each of us saw Clann na Poblachta as answering our own special needs. The ex-IRA men simply wanted an end to partition and a united Ireland. I wanted our health services restructured. Jack McQuillan, another radical, hoped for a serious land and agricultural policy.'

Being part of the inter-party government meant that Clann surrendered some of its radical edge, especially given its association with the more conservative Fine Gael. In addition, power gave Fine Gael a new lease of life from which it was to go on and rebuild itself. By joining the inter-party government Clann was aligned with all the anti-Fianna Fáil parties. Within a few years political life had settled back into two groupings: Fianna Fáil supporters and those who did not endorse the dominant party but backed Fine Gael.

At the 1951 general election, Fianna Fáil was successful at winning back some of those who had voted Clann at the previous general election. In a sense Clann had won discontented supporters from all parties in 1948. It was an electoral protest against the political establishment. Having given the established parties a fright, thereafter the electorate returned to its familiar voting pattern.

Clann never regrouped after the split of 1951. The loss of men of the calibre of Noël Browne, Noel Hartnett and Jack McQuillan hit the fledgling party hard. Without them the drive was taken out of the party. It was then Seán MacBride's party, given the dominance of his personality over those who remained. Throughout the 1950s Clann played the role of nagging critic in the corner - identifying issues and then following them until they were taken up by the main parties. Clann can be credited with placing economic planning on the political agenda, a fact that is often overlooked. In addition, the party to its end placed great emphasis on the need to achieve equality in the education system.

Michael Gallagher has noted that one of the most remarkable features of the Irish electoral system is the high retention rate of transfers by Fianna Fáil. On average over

80 per cent of transferred votes from Fianna Fáil candidates have gone to other Fianna Fáil candidates that are available to receive transfers.

Looking at the transfer of lower preference votes can be used to gauge how well a party is organised. Party solidarity can be measured by considering the proportion of transfers which remain within a party at election time. A high solidarity is a sign of a party organisation that is characterised by efficiency and vitality. A lower solidarity indicates a weaker organisation, with candidates relying on votes on their own merits as much as on the party's appeal.

The level of solidarity for smaller parties would generally be lower. Indeed, the solidarity level would be expected to become weaker as the party grows older. This is the case with Clann na Poblachta. The party's solidarity level declines as the party's national strength declines. Clann's rate in 1948 was fairly high for a new party. Nearly 70 per cent of its transfers remained within the party fold where possible in 1948. However, this had fallen to just under 34 per cent by 1954.

The following table illustrates how after the 1954 general election Clann had become little more than a grouping of independents campaigning only nominally on a party label. Yet as a new party entering the Irish political system it achieved much more than the vast majority of other parties which have attempted to challenge the Fianna Fáil-Fine Gael-Labour dominance. Indeed, it was not until the Progressive Democrats went into government with Fianna Fáil in 1989 that Irish politics again witnessed an upheaval in established patterns such as it had done in 1948.

Clann's Electoral Performance 1948-65				
General Election	Candidates	Seats Won	Total Vote	% Total Vote
1948	93	10	174,823	13.2
1951	26	2	54,210	4.1
1954	20	3	51,069	3.8
1957	12	1	20,632	1.7
1961	5	1	13,170	1.1
1965	4	1	9,427	0.8

SELECT BIBLIOGRAPHY

In addition to various Clann na Poblachta publications, use has also been made of Oireachtas proceedings as well as national and local papers. These are referred to, where appropriate, throughout the text.

Browne, Noël, *Against the tide*, 1986.

Browne, Vincent, *The Magill Book of Irish Politics*, 1981.

Carty, R. K., *Party and parish pump: electoral politics in Ireland*, 1981.

Chubb, Basil, *Cabinet Government in Ireland*, 1974.

Coakley, John, 'Minor Parties in Irish Political Life, 1922-1989' in *Economic and Social Review*, 3, 1990.

Coakley, John and Michael Gallagher, *Politics in the Republic of Ireland*, 1992.

Fanning, Ronan, *The Irish Department of Finance*, 1978.

Farrell, Brian, *Chairman or Chief, The Role of Taoiseach in Irish Government*, 1971.

Gallagher, Michael, *Political Parties in the Republic of Ireland*, 1985.

———, *The Irish Labour Party in Transition 1957-72*, 1978.

———, 'Party solidarity, exclusivity and inter-party relationships in Ireland, 1922-1977: the evidence of transfers', in *Economic and Social Review*, 10, 1978.

———, 'The impact of lower preference votes on Irish parliamentary elections, 1922-1977' in *Economic and Social*

Review, 11, 1979.

Lee, J. J., *Ireland 1912-1985*, 1989.

Mair, P., *The Changing Irish Party System* ,1987.

Manning, Maurice, *Irish Political Parties: An Introduction*, 1972.

Maye, Brian, *Fine Gael,* 1993.

Nowlan, K. B. and T. D. Williams (eds.), *Ireland in the War Years and After*, 1969.

O'Keeffe, P. D., 'The origins and development of Clann na Poblachta', unpublished MA thesis, UCC, 1981.

Ward, Margaret, *Maud Gonne, A Biography*, 1990.

INDEX